Government's Greatest Achievements

FROM CIVIL RIGHTS TO HOMELAND DEFENSE

Paul C. Light

BROOKINGS INSTITUTION PRESS
Washington, D.C.

Copyright © 2002
THE BROOKINGS INSTITUTION
1775 Massachusetts Avenue, N.W., Washington, D.C. 20036
www.brookings.edu

Library of Congress Cataloging-in-Publication data
Light, Paul Charles
  Government's greatest achievements: from civil rights to homeland defense /
Paul C. Light
     p.   cm.
Includes bibliographical references (p.   ) and index.
  ISBN 0-8157-0604-9 (alk. paper)
  1. Political planning—United States. 2. United States—Politics and
government—1945–1989. 3. United States—Politics and government—
1989– I. Title.
JK468.P64 L54 2002   2002000914
320'.6'097309045—dc21   CIP

                    9 8 7 6 5 4 3 2 1

The paper used in this publication meets minimum requirements of the
American National Standard for Information Sciences—Permanence of Paper
          for Printed Library Materials: ANSI Z39.48-1992.

                    Typeset in Adobe Garamond

   Composition and text design by Circle Graphics, Columbia, Maryland

       Printed by R. R. Donnelley and Sons, Harrisonburg, Virginia

Contents

Preface

This book reflects a three-year effort to chronicle the federal government's successes and failures over the past half-century. Its most significant contribution to the field may reside less in its rankings of what academics see as government's greatest achievements and more in its painstaking analysis of major legislation showing just how much the federal government endeavored to accomplish in the past fifty years.

This analysis is based on a significant new approach to understanding how Congress sets priorities for government. Instead of focusing on individual laws such as the Medicare Act or Marshall Plan, my researchers and I have examined groups of laws designed to solve specific problems, such as improving access to health care or rebuilding Europe after World War II. Like David Mayhew's seminal book *Divided We Govern*, this analysis shows that government is most successful when Congress and the presidency work together in a bipartisan, bi-institutional manner. It is a critically important finding for this moment in time. If this nation is to win the war on terrorism and rebuild homeland security, its national institutions must find and hold common ground.

This analysis also shows that the federal government is quite capable of achieving important goals if given consistent direction and support for doing so. The federal government's greatest achievements of the past fifty years came on issues where Congress and the presidency were clear on both the means and ends. The federal government has done its best work when the nation's leaders have identified a clear problem and amassed the political will to pursue tangible action. Conversely, the federal government has created its greatest disappointments when the nation's leaders have sent mixed signals about whether and how to solve a problem and/or have been unwilling to commit the resources needed for progress.

This book was written with a generous grant from the Ford Foundation. I am particularly grateful for the insights and encouragement of senior program officer Michael Lipsky, who helped solidify the idea for the project. I am also indebted to my research team, which included Judith Labiner, deputy director, Center for Public Service; Mary McIntosh, vice president, Princeton Survey Research Associates; and Michael Wiesenfelder, research assistant. Thanks go also to both Charles O. Jones for his comments and the anonymous reviewers whose suggestions clearly improved this book. Last, the expert copyediting skills brought to the manuscript by Starr Belsky were much appreciated.

Government's Greatest Achievements

1

Aiming High, Trying Hard

Greatest Endeavors of the Past Half-Century

Looking back at the events of September 11, 2001, it is easy to wonder whether the United States will ever return to normal. The terrorist attacks on New York and Washington changed American life forever, fundamentally altering just what "normal" means. Americans will always remember where they were when they heard the news about the World Trade Center and Pentagon tragedies.

As Americans look for reassurance in this era of vulnerability, at least some can be found in the federal government's extraordinary record of achievement over the past half century. Despite what may have seemed like insurmountable odds at the time, the federal government helped rebuild Europe after World War II, conquered polio and a host of other life-threatening diseases, faced down communism, attacked racial discrimination in the voting booth, housing, and the public square, and reduced poverty among the nation's elderly to its lowest levels in modern history.

If assassinations, urban riots, the Vietnam War, the Watergate scandal, Iran hostage taking, the first New York Trade Center bombings in 1993, presidential resignations and impeachment, and stock market crashes were not enough to prevent progress on these extraordinary endeavors, neither will the acts of terrorism. To the extent a nation's greatness is measured by what its government has accomplished through good times and bad, Americans can have great confidence that the federal government will succeed in strengthening homeland defense. Perhaps that is why trust in government surged by nearly 30 percent in the wake of the attacks, reaching levels not seen since 1968 in the midst of the Vietnam War. Perhaps that is also why confidence in federal employees to do their jobs also hit historic highs. Americans know that there are few problems that cannot be solved with determination and grit.

Some of this success has come through great laws such as the 1965 Medicare Act, which created a new health care program for the nation's elderly, or audacious efforts such as the Apollo space program, which helped the United States win the race to the moon. However, most of the success has been achieved and sustained through collections of smaller, often unheralded laws to clean the air and water, reduce disease, feed the hungry, or protect wild lands and rivers. America rarely conquers its problems in an instant. Rather, it tends to wear problems down, year after year, law after law, until victory is won.

The proof is in more than 500 major laws passed since 1946. Having emerged victorious from World War II and a decade-long economic depression, Congress called upon the federal government to tackle an agenda of concerns worthy of the world's greatest democracy. Over the last half of the twentieth century, the federal government was asked to advance human rights abroad, increase homeownership, expand voting rights, improve air and water quality, reduce the threat of nuclear war, create open housing for all races, protect endangered species and the wilderness, reduce hunger, defeat communism, and build the interstate highway system. Although there have been failures mixed in with the success, Congress has never been reluctant to ask the federal government to tackle tough, difficult problems, and the federal government has mostly succeeded in response.

In this era of promises to create smaller, more limited government, Americans often forget that the federal government has amassed a distinguished record of endeavor that no other sector, private or nonprofit, could create on its own. Perhaps that is why President Bush took such pains after the terrorist attacks to reassure the nation that the federal government would be open for business the next day.

The United States is now facing another seemingly insurmountable problem in the form of international terrorism. By early 2002 it had already produced enough federal action to make this one of the most intensive endeavors of recent history. Congress passed the USA PATRIOT Act in October, giving the president sweeping authority to investigate and prevent terrorism, and created a new federal Transportation Security Agency in November to tighten security at the nation's airports. At the same time, the president ordered thousands of troops and aircraft to Afghanistan to topple the Taliban government that had harbored Osama bin Laden and his al-Qaida network of terrorists.

However, as of early 2002 the question is not whether the effort to strengthen homeland defense and battle terrorism abroad will be one of the federal government's greatest endeavors of the new century. Rather, the question for most Americans is whether the United States will actually achieve results. Will airports become safer? Will bin Laden be brought to justice? Can government prevent future attacks? Moreover, as the events of September 11 fade from memory, it is not clear whether homeland defense and the war on terrorism will remain high priorities far into the future. How much money is Congress really willing to spend on domestic security? How long will Americans tolerate long lines at the airport? How long will the president stay focused on homeland defense?

These questions focus on the three major terms in this book: endeavor, achievement, and priority. An *endeavor* involves the government's effort to solve some problem such as racial discrimination, air pollution, terrorism, or poverty. An *achievement* entails government progress in actually solving a problem, for example, by reducing discrimination, preventing pollution, strengthening security, or lowering poverty. Finally, a *priority* involves choices about how hard the government should work on an endeavor in the future. Chapter 1 of this book focuses on the federal government's greatest endeavors of the past fifty years; chapter 2, on what America's leading historians and political scientists see as the government's greatest achievements of the past fifty years; and chapter 3, on what economists, historians, political scientists, and sociologists believe are the most important priorities for the future.

This chapter explores government's greatest endeavors by defining terms, sorting individual laws into broader endeavors, and searching for patterns in what government has tried to do these past fifty years. Readers are cautioned that the term *greatest* does not mean the best, most successful, or even most important. Rather, it refers to the problems that the federal government tried hardest to solve.

THE ANATOMY OF AN ENDEAVOR

Americans tend to focus on government laws, orders, and decisions whenever they think about what the federal government does. That is how the media and many experts think of government, too. Congress passes laws, presidents issue orders, and federal courts make decisions. Survey researchers rarely ask Americans what they think about the federal government's overall effort to reduce poverty among the elderly, improve drinking water safety, or protect the wilderness, for example. They ask instead about public confidence in the future of programs such as Social Security, fears about specific problems such as airplane hijackings, or proposed solutions such as oil drilling in the Alaskan wildlife preserve.

Much as individual laws, orders, and decisions matter to what the federal government does, they are best viewed as the building blocks of larger endeavors to solve problems. Even great laws such as the 1935 Social Security Act, the 1964 Civil Rights Act, the 1965 Medicare Act, and the Clean Air and Clean Water Acts have been amended repeatedly over time to broaden their coverage and protect past gains. Just as Rome was not built in a day, federal progress on the great problems of history is rarely found in a single law or decision.

There are three parts to every government endeavor chronicled in this chapter. First, every endeavor involves a problem. Some problems are more difficult to solve, while others appear to be easier. Some problems are more important, while others are judged less significant. Finally, some problems can only be solved if the federal government takes the lead, while others are better tackled by state and local governments, the nonprofit sector, private groups, or individual citizens and families.

Second, every endeavor involves a solution. Some solutions can be found in a law or laws such as the Voting Rights Act, the Housing and Community Development Act, or the antiterrorism laws passed in the wake of the New York and Washington attacks. Other solutions can be found in Supreme Court decisions such as *Brown* v. *Topeka Board of Education*, which abolished racial discrimination in the public schools. Still others can result from presidential orders. By definition an endeavor demands tangible, not symbolic, action.

Some problems involve more than one kind of solution, however. On the one hand, the federal government strengthened the nation's highway system by doing the same thing over and over: building thousands and thousands of miles of highways, bridges, and roads. On the other hand, Congress has never been quite sure what it wants to do about immigration. It has passed laws to invite illegal immigrants to stay and laws to force them to leave, laws to tighten the nation's borders and laws to let more immigrants in.

Third, every endeavor involves some level of effort. The level of effort can be measured in a variety of ways: the number of laws passed, pages of regulation written, amount of money spent, or number of employees hired. Great endeavors require more than great intentions: they usually require sustained action over time.

WHAT GOVERNMENT HAS TRIED TO DO

There are several ways to identify the federal government's greatest endeavors. One is to search the federal budget for the largest programs. Another is to read and count the number of pages devoted to a specific problem in the *Code of Federal Regulations*, which records the rules that the federal government adopts to implement the laws, decisions, and orders given by the three branches of government. Still another way is to track the number of federal employees involved in solving a particular problem.

This book is based on reading the federal statute books, which record every law passed by Congress, signed by the president, and deemed constitutional by the federal courts. Not only are laws the "stem cell," or starting point, for almost everything that government does, they are easy to identify and count. Scholars know exactly how many laws have been passed in every two-year Congress, what those laws were intended to do, and whether those laws are major or minor, substantive or symbolic. Moreover, to the extent that Congress is serious when it tries to solve a problem through the legislative process, the *Congressional Quarterly Almanac* provides an easily accessible source of information on the most important laws.

The *Congressional Quarterly Almanac* is considered more than just the final word on what Congress and the president try to do. Its annual summary of the major legislation enacted and signed into law is considered the authoritative source on which laws are important. Because laws determine the number of federal rules, size of the federal budgets, and number of federal employees, they are the logical place to start in building a list of the government's greatest endeavors.

Congressional Quarterly is not the only resource on the major laws of the past half-century, however. Yale University political scientist David Mayhew has been working on his own list of major legislation for the past two decades, adding new laws at the end of each two-year Congress.[1] Mayhew's list of more than 300 laws is based on two sweeps of history, the first a careful reading of the *New York Times* and *Washington Post* at the end of each year to see what the two newspapers covered as the most important laws of the year, and

1. David R. Mayhew, *Divided We Govern: Party Control, Lawmaking, and Investigations, 1946–1990* (Yale University Press, 1991).

the second a careful reading of deeper histories by political scientists, historians, and other scholars to see which of those laws passed the test of time as truly important.

Using Mayhew's list as an anchor, this study of government's greatest endeavors is based on a further reading of every *Congressional Quarterly Almanac* and year-end *Congressional Quarterly Weekly* summary from 1944 through 1999. Researchers looked not only for the accomplishments of Congress as a whole but also for legislation that might have been overlooked by the press or scholars, or could be judged a significant legislative accomplishment in its own field. That deeper analysis produced a list of more than 540 major laws passed over the last half-century, dealing with virtually every domestic and foreign problem imaginable. Some of the laws are instantly recognizable whereas others are only known to the small number of experts in specific fields. But whether familiar or obscure, these laws show just how much the federal government tried to do between the end of World War II and the inauguration of President George W. Bush in 2001.

FROM LAWS TO ENDEAVORS

It is one thing to identify the major laws of the past half century, however, and quite another to combine those individual laws into broad endeavors. The first step is to identify the problem each law tried to solve. As already noted, Congress has asked the federal government to solve just about every problem imaginable, from promoting the arts at home to promoting democracy abroad, protecting the elderly from poverty to protecting the world from communism, expanding access to education for America's children to expanding humanitarian relief for the world's poor.

From 1944 through 2001, for example, Congress passed twenty-seven major laws to protect and expand civil rights in the United States. Some of those laws dealt with expanding the right to vote by eliminating practices such as the literacy test and poll tax; others focused on ending discrimination against people of color, women, and the disabled; and still others aimed to end discrimination in public places such as bus stations, restaurants, and hotels. Although all of these laws dealt with discrimination, there were at least three specific problems Congress tried to solve: voting discrimination, workplace discrimination, and discrimination in public accommodations such as hotels and housing.

During the same period, Congress passed more than eighty laws to protect the environment and ensure an adequate supply of energy. Some of those laws dealt with protecting endangered species, some with protecting the wilderness; other laws involved the national energy supply or cleanup of hazardous waste. Although all of the laws had a very broad aim, Congress tried to solve at least six different problems: endangered species, loss of wilderness, hazardous waste, energy shortages, air pollution, and water pollution.

The second step in developing a list of greatest endeavors is to identify the federal government's greatest, or most intensive, efforts of the past fifty years. There is nothing magical about this: one simply determines how hard Congress asked the federal government to work in solving the given problem. It is easy to see, for example, that for the past fifty years, Congress has asked the federal government to devote more time, money, and employees to strengthen the nation's highway system than to develop the nation's great river valleys, or that Congress has expended more legislative energy to promote space exploration than to protect privacy. This does not mean that developing river valleys and protecting privacy are unimportant, trivial goals. Rather, it demonstrates that all government endeavors do not involve the same amount of effort, whether measured by the amount of money, time, legislative attention, federal employees, rules, or bureaucracy devoted to each cause.

Most of the fifty greatest endeavors discussed below involve tightly focused legislative action to solve clearly defined problems. Thus the Civil Rights Act of 1964 fits naturally in the effort to attack workplace discrimination as addressed by the Age Discrimination Act of 1967 and the Americans with Disabilities Act of 1990. Likewise, the Omnibus Crime Control and Safe Streets Act of 1968—along with its 1970, 1984, and 1994 amendments—fits in tightly with the effort to reduce crime expressed in the Organized Crime

Control Act of 1970. In another example, the World War II Bretton Woods Agreement, which created a new international financial system, fits naturally with the campaign to expand world trade as addressed by the Trade Expansion Act of 1962, the Trade and Tariff Act of 1964, and the North American Free Trade Agreement (NAFTA) of 1993.

However, some of the fifty greatest endeavors involve less coherent collections of laws. The legislative effort to improve mass transportation includes a broad range of laws covering everything from the creation of the Amtrak passenger rail system to more federal funding for urban mass transit, while the effort to control immigration involves four contradictory laws that share little more than the word "immigration" in their titles.

There are lessons to be learned from the lack of coherence, however. The lack of consensus on whether and how to address the problems of immigration and urban mass transit, for example, is one explanation for the general lack of progress in either area. In contrast, the general consensus on whether and how to end racial discrimination and reduce poverty among older Americans is one explanation for the great progress toward solving both problems.

CHARACTERISTICS OF THE LIST

There are three unique aspects of the inventory discussed below. First, some laws contribute to more than one endeavor, particularly when those laws involve omnibus, or large-scale, packages of ideas.

The 1964 Civil Rights Act is one such law. The act banned discrimination on the basis of race, color, sex, religion, or national origin, whether by employers or labor unions, in businesses or in hotels, restaurants, theaters, gas stations, and all other public accommodations. It provided federal money to help integrate the public schools, allowed the federal government to withhold federal money from organizations such as colleges and universities that discriminate on the basis of race, color, gender, religion, or national origin. It also created the U.S. Equal Employment Opportunity Commission to review complaints about workplace discrimination. As such, the act contributes to at least two endeavors discussed below: ending work-place discrimination and opening public accommodations. As this book suggests later, it may well be the single most important domestic law enacted over the past fifty years.

The 1947 National Security Act is another multiendeavor law. The act created the modern Department of Defense by merging the old Departments of War, Army, and Navy with the newly created Department of the Air Force under a unified command. It also created the Central Intelligence Agency (CIA) and the National Security Council (NSC), both of which are intimately involved in U.S. foreign policy. Thus the act contributes to two endeavors discussed below: containing communism and strengthening the national defense. It may well be the single most important foreign policy law passed over the past fifty years.

Second, readers may wonder why highly visible endeavors such as enhancing peace in the Middle East or protecting civil liberties such as freedom of the press and religion are not on the following list. The answer is that this is a book about laws, not executive action or court decisions. Notwithstanding all the time presidents have spent on the Middle East and all the Supreme Court decisions on civil liberties, Congress did not enact enough major legislation for either area to make the list of government's greatest endeavors.

This is not to suggest that the presidency or the federal judiciary is somehow irrelevant to government's greatest endeavors. Indeed, both play a significant role in both proposing and enforcing the laws that form the endeavors discussed below. At the front end of the legislative process, presidents often set the agenda of national concern by proposing laws to Congress through their budgets, treaty negotiations with other nations, and State of the Union addresses, while the federal courts often stimulate legislative action by taking the lead in defining a problem such as racial discrimination. At the implementation stage of the process, presidents are responsible for overseeing the day-to-day operations of government, while the courts enforce the laws.

Third, readers will note that strengthening homeland defense and the war on terrorism are not on the list of government's greatest endeavors of the past fifty years. That is because the war on terrorism did not begin in earnest until the first World Trade Center bombings in 1993 and only intensified after the September 11 attacks. Congress passed several smaller scale laws to fight terrorism prior to 2001, but none made the *Congressional Quarterly* list of major legislation in 2000. Although homeland defense and the war on terrorism certainly make the list of government's greatest endeavors of today, they were not on the list before September 11, 2001.

GOVERNMENT'S FIFTY GREATEST ENDEAVORS

Congress asked the federal government to solve a truly remarkable assortment of problems between World War II and the end of the twentieth century. The fifty endeavors reviewed here reflect its most intensive efforts to improve life both at home and abroad; some of these were under way before 1945 and almost all continue today. To the extent a society is measured at least in part by what it asks its government to do, Americans can be very proud indeed. (See appendix A for a basic list of the endeavors and some of the action Congress took in support of them.)

▉ Advance Human Rights and Provide Humanitarian Relief

Congress has been promoting human rights and helping victims of natural disasters through legislation ever since it ratified the United Nations charter in 1945. Having started with 51 members, the UN now consists of 185 countries, including all of the former members of the Soviet Union. By providing a safe place to resolve very difficult world problems, the United States and its allies hoped that dialogue and understanding would replace military power and war as a basis for making decisions.

Congress continued the effort to help other nations when it passed the Refugee Relief Act of 1953, approving the admission of 214,000 refugees, mostly from Europe. It acted again to help refugees when it passed the Migration and Refugee Assistance Act of 1962, which provided almost $4 billion in foreign economic and

military aid. Congress also sought to end racial separatism in South
Africa by passing the 1986 Comprehensive Anti-Apartheid Act,
authorized the use of U.S. troops in the Somalia peacekeeping mission, and approved the air war over Kosovo in the spring of 1999.

*Seven major laws or treaty ratifications have supported this
endeavor.*

▪ Contain Communism

Congress began fighting the spread of communism almost immediately after World War II when it endorsed President Harry Truman's grand strategy of containment, promising to defend freedom
wherever it was threatened. Part of implementing this Truman Doctrine involved helping democratic allies that bordered the collection
of communist states called the Soviet Union. Congress approved
$400 million for aid to Greece and Turkey in 1946, for example, and
ratified the North Atlantic Treaty creating the North Atlantic Treaty
Organization (NATO) in 1949, which pulled together the nations
of Western Europe and the United States into a military and economic alliance. Despite these earlier efforts, mainland China fell to
the communists in 1949, and North Korea invaded South Korea in
1950.

The North Korean invasion provided a particularly significant
test of the grand strategy of containment. The United States
responded with a full-scale military intervention that cost 54,000
U.S. lives and another 100,000 casualties in a war that ended in
stalemate. A decade later the United States became engaged in Vietnam. Convinced that the fall of South Vietnam would lead to the fall
of Southeast Asia, tipping a long chain of dominoes that would eventually lead to the fall of its own government, the United States
entered what would become its longest and most unpopular war.
Starting with a handful of military advisers in 1959 and rising to a
force of more than 500,000 troops in 1965, the Vietnam War also
ended in stalemate after the loss of 58,000 lives.

Four major laws have supported this endeavor.

Control Immigration

For 200 years Congress has been trying to strike the right balance between encouraging legal immigration while protecting the nation's borders against illegal entry, including that by terrorists. Congress passed the Immigration and Nationality Act of 1952 that established a new quota system limiting immigration from each area of the world; it then amended the act in 1965 to lighten the restrictions.

Congress continued moving the pendulum with the 1986 Immigration Control Act. On the one hand, the act gave amnesty to all illegal aliens already residing in the United States by making them citizens. On the other hand, the act increased the penalties for hiring an illegal alien and strengthened the U.S. Immigration and Naturalization Service and its border patrol as a bulwark against illegal entry. In 1990 Congress approved a substantial increase in immigration, including a new category for workers with hard-to-find skills such as computer programming.

Four major laws have supported this endeavor.

Develop and Renew Impoverished Communities

Congress has been working to reduce urban and rural poverty since the mid-1940s when it twice amended the Rural Electrification Act to expand rural access to electricity and telephones. The tone of the federal government's work to improve poor communities changed dramatically in 1961 when Congress passed the Area Redevelopment Act to help poor Americans in the poorest sections of the Appalachian Mountains that run 2,200 miles from Mount Katahdin in Maine to Springer Mountain in Georgia. The act authorized $400 million for rural development loans for areas that had experienced high unemployment over the three preceding years. Congress passed the 1961 Housing Act two months later, including $2 billion for urban renewal efforts.

Congress expanded this part of President Lyndon Johnson's War on Poverty when it passed the 1965 Appalachian Regional

Development Act, which covered the entire state of West Virginia and parts of eleven other Appalachian states. The bill provided more than $1 billion for economic development, road construction, and an assortment of vocational programs, water programs, and even a program for filling and sealing old coal mines. Congress also passed the 1966 Democratic Cities and Metropolitan Development Act, the 1972 Rural Development Act, and the 2000 Community Renewal and New Markets Act, all of which funded expanded aid to poor communities.

Nine major laws have supported this endeavor.

▓ Devolve Responsibilities to the States

Since the 1970s Congress has made a host of efforts to return power to state and local governments through what is often called the new federalism, a term President Richard Nixon coined in the early 1970s to describe his plans to shift federal responsibilities and dollars back to the states and localities. However, Nixon did believe that welfare and environmental protection were best handled by the national government, in part because the states could not be trusted to set a reasonable minimum level of welfare benefits and in part because many environmental problems cross state lines.

Congress implemented Nixon's new federalism through two major programs. The first was a new form of national support for the states that replaced a vast array of existing categorical grants for community development, job training, and education with giant block grants that states could use with fewer strings attached as long as the money was spent for the broad purposes intended. The second was a new national funding program called general revenue sharing, which was designed to give states a portion of the national tax dollars. Begun in 1972 and ended in 1986, revenue sharing was an effort to reduce the national budget deficit. The program sent states and localities an average of over $6 billion a year even as the amount of money devoted to block grants continued to increase steadily.

Nixon's ideas for returning power to the states are still active. They were adopted as part of the Contract with America agenda by the new Republican House majority in 1994, where they came to be known as the "Newt Federalism" in honor of Republican House Speaker Newt Gingrich, a contemporary advocate of states' rights. Congress sent billions in funding back to the states under the 1972 State and Local Fiscal Assistance Act, which is more commonly known as revenue sharing, and tried to reduce burdens on states through the 1995 Unfunded Mandate Reform Act, which requires Congress to pay more attention to any proposed law that establishes an unfunded mandate.

Three major laws have supported this endeavor.

Enhance Consumer Protection

Congress has been trying to protect consumers from unsafe products since the early 1900s, when it passed the landmark Food and Drug Act that prohibited interstate commerce in misbranded food, drinks, and drugs. In 1951 Congress expanded that law by setting uniform standards for over-the-counter drugs such as aspirin and cold medicines, and did so again in 1962 when it required every drug manufacturer to register its drugs with the government.

Congress also pushed for greater honesty in labeling of food and drugs under a number of laws, starting with the 1965 Federal Cigarette Labeling and Advertising Act, which required all cigarette cartons and packages to contain the label "Warning: The Surgeon General Has Determined That Cigarette Smoking Is Dangerous to Your Health." Congress continued to demand greater honesty under the 1966 Food Safety and Labeling Act, which required more detailed information on the content of packaged foods, and the 1966 Child Protection Act, which extended labeling requirements to cover dangerous toys and children's products. These laws acquired greater muscle in 1972 when Congress created the Consumer Product Safety Commission to enforce standards for consumer products other than food, drugs, firearms, and motor vehicles, which are all products covered by other government agencies such as the Food and Drug Administration. In 1990 Congress further extended truth-in-labeling by passing the Nutrition Labeling and Education Act, requiring food producers and distributors to provide information on the amount of fat, saturated fat, cholesterol, sodium, sugar, fiber, and protein while prohibiting producers from making nutritional claims, such as "low fat," without evidence.

Thirteen major laws have supported this endeavor.

▪ Enhance the Nation's Health Care Infrastructure

Congress has invested billions over the past fifty years building and modernizing America's hospitals and health research centers. Much of that funding was funneled through the 1946 Hospital Survey and Construction Act, which authorized $75 million a year for construction of public and nonprofit hospitals. In 1949 Congress doubled the program's funding, encouraging much of the hospital construction that is still part of the nation's health care infrastructure today, and under the Community Health Services and Facilities Act of 1961, it increased federal grants to the states for the construction of nursing homes and outpatient facilities for the aged and chronically ill. The federal government became involved in building mental health facilities under the 1963 Mental Retardation Facilities Construction Act, which was expanded in 1970 with increased federal funding. Congress also ordered the federal government and the states to work together on health planning in 1966 and again in 1974 by providing health planning grants and by creating the National Council on Health Planning and Development. By 1974 it also changed funding priorities under the 1946 Hospital Survey and Construction Act to favor modernization of old facilities over new construction.

Eleven major laws have supported this endeavor.

▪ Enhance Workplace Safety

Congress has been trying to protect workers from accidents and unsafe working conditions since the early 1900s when it asked the federal government to regulate the meat packing industry. Congress expanded the effort to coal miners under the 1952 Mine Safety Act, which gave the federal government authority to shut down dangerous mines. In an attempt to combat black lung disease, Congress amended the law in 1969 to set limits on the amount of coal dust allowed in mine shafts.

Although these two laws did reduce mine accidents and black lung disease, they did nothing to help other workers. To protect all workers, Congress passed the sweeping 1970 Occupational Safety and Health Act, which established the principle that employers should take all reasonable measures to protect their employees. The law created a new federal Occupational Safety and Health Administration (OSHA), which was given the authority to set and enforce standards covering a long list of threats to workplace safety. OSHA was also given the authority to inspect workplaces and issue citations for immediate action.

Three major laws have supported this endeavor.

■ Ensure an Adequate Energy Supply

Over the past half century, Congress has asked the federal government to pursue three major energy goals. The first goal was set in the 1940s when Congress passed the 1946 Atomic Energy Act, which established the Atomic Energy Commission (AEC) to both regulate and promote the use of nuclear power for civilian and military use. Congress gave the AEC authority to grant licenses to domestic nuclear power producers in 1954 and also guaranteed up to $500 million in liability coverage in the event of an accident at a federally licensed power plant.

At the same time, Congress also encouraged development of traditional sources of energy, including oil, natural gas, and electricity. It funded three new power-generating dams on the Colorado River in 1956 and authorized construction of a pipeline to tap into the vast northern Alaskan oil reserves in 1973. In addition, Congress encouraged energy conservation by establishing new fuel efficiency requirements under the 1975 Energy Policy and Conservation Act.

In 1974, recognizing the difficulty of running these programs through a patchwork of federal agencies, Congress divided the AEC into the Nuclear Regulatory Commission and the Energy Research and Development Administration. The former was given the responsibility to regulate the nuclear industry, while the latter was designed in part to expand the industry and other sources of energy. Facing continued gasoline and heating oil shortages in 1977, Congress again reorganized energy policy by creating the Department of Energy in 1978, thus responding to President Jimmy Carter's declaration of the "moral equivalent of war" on energy shortages.

Fourteen major laws have supported this endeavor.

Ensure Safe Food and Drinking Water

Congress has been protecting citizens from tainted food and impure drinking water for more than a century, but its efforts became much more aggressive in 1947 when it required that all pesticides be registered with the Department of Agriculture and gave the federal government authority to ban all unregistered poisons, as well as any that did not list the product name, manufacturer's address, warnings, and the proper antidote on the packaging. Congress expanded these protections in 1964 and again in 1972, when it required registration of all pesticides with the Environmental Protection Agency (EPA), which had been created in 1970 to coordinate most environmental laws.

Congress passed many other laws to protect citizens from tainted food and drinking water. In 1957 it directed the Department of Agriculture to inspect poultry, in 1967 it strengthened existing meat standards, and in 1968 it toughened the poultry standards by giving the federal government power to oversee state inspection programs. Congress also passed the 1974 Safe Drinking Water Act to protect citizens from chemicals and pesticides that migrate into drinking water.

Nine major laws have supported this endeavor.

Expand Homeownership

Congressional efforts to expand homeownership began before the end of World War II with passage of the 1944 Servicemen's Readjustment Act, or "GI Bill," which gave returning soldiers access to low-cost home loans. Under the original act, veterans could apply for loans of up to $7,500. Today, veterans can apply for loans up to $240,000, depending on their income.

Home loans were useless if no homes were for sale, however. With the nation mired in a housing shortage, Congress passed the 1950 Housing Act, which provided additional loan guarantees for all Americans, thus stimulating a housing boom. Further shortages in areas near defense plants prompted Congress to pass the Defense Housing Act of 1951, which provided even more federal funding to stimulate construction in those areas.

By 1965 federal housing programs had become so numerous and important that Congress created the Department of Housing and Urban Development (HUD). Although veterans' home loans remained with the Veterans Administration (now Department of Veterans Affairs), HUD became the host of a number of programs to stimulate community renewal, urban development, and low-income housing construction. Congress also encouraged the purchase of homes by allowing homeowners to deduct the full cost of interest payments from their annual taxes, thereby improving the attraction of buying, not renting, homes.

Nine major laws have supported this endeavor.

▓ Expand Foreign Markets for U.S. Goods

Congress has been regulating imports and exports since the time of the Revolutionary War, which itself was sparked in part by unfair British taxes on imports, such as tea and sugar. After 150 years of protecting its own industries, the U.S. turned toward free trade as a way to promote exports abroad. Congress embraced free trade by ratifying a number of agreements: the 1944 Bretton Woods Agreement, which established a new world currency system; the 1947 General Agreement on Tariffs and Trade (GATT), which created a framework for resolving trade disputes and promoting free trade; and the 1961 Organization for Economic Cooperation and Development, which created a trade alliance consisting of the United States and eighteen European countries. All of these reforms were designed to stabilize the world financial markets in the wake of World War II while encouraging the lowering of trade barriers.

Congress overhauled the nation's trade laws in 1962 under the Trade Expansion Act, which gave the president a five-year authority to cut tariffs on imports and exports by 50 percent. The Trade Act of 1974 extended that authority, enabled the president to assign most favored nation trading status to certain countries, and created the Office of Special Trade Representative in the Executive Office of the President. Congress has generally remained steady in promoting free trade. For example, despite strong opposition from organized labor, which feared a loss of jobs to Mexico, Congress ratified the North American Free Trade Agreement in 1993, lifting all tariff barriers among the United States, Mexico, and Canada by 2008.

Thirteen major laws have supported this endeavor.

Expand Job Training and Placement

Since the Great Depression of the 1930s, Congress has been helping unemployed Americans find work. It restarted the endeavor after World War II when it passed the Employment Act of 1946, which set a goal of full employment for all citizens. Although the act did not contain any funding, it pledged the federal government to help every American "able, willing, and seeking work." Congress followed up in 1953 by creating the Small Business Administration to help small businesses attain government contracts, loans, and disaster relief.

With the Manpower Development and Training Act of 1962, Congress involved the federal government in job training through a three-year program to help retrain workers who had lost their jobs due to new technology. The Job Corps was created two years later, based on rural "conservation camps" and other training centers to give high school dropouts access to basic education and vocational training. Congress continued to expand federal training programs under the Comprehensive Employment and Training Act (CETA) in 1973, which provided federal dollars for public service jobs around the country. Beset by fraud and public opposition to federally funded jobs, CETA was replaced in 1982 by the Job Training Partnership Act.

Twelve major laws have supported this endeavor.

Expand the Right to Vote

The right to vote was granted to former slaves under the Fifteenth Amendment in 1870 and to women under the Nineteenth Amendment in 1920. However, it was not guaranteed until the 1960s when Congress passed the Twenty-Fourth Amendment, which outlawed the use of poll taxes or other taxes as a condition for voting in federal elections, and the landmark 1965 Voting Rights Act, which prohibited the use of literacy tests as a condition of voting and authorized federal registrars to register thousands of black voters across the South. Although the 1965 act is considered the breakthrough law, Congress actually started work on voting rights in 1957 when it cre-

MATT HERRON/TAKE STOCK

Marching toward conflict, 1965. Marchers leave the city of Selma en route to a confrontation with Alabama state police on what would become known as "Bloody Sunday."

ated the Civil Rights Commission, which had the power to investigate allegations that some Americans were being deprived of their right to vote due to their race, religion, or ethnicity. Congress also passed the Civil Rights Act of 1960 that increased penalties for violent acts designed to stop individuals from voting because of their race or color.

Congress again expanded the right to vote when it ratified the Twenty-Sixth Amendment in 1971 that gave eighteen- to twenty-year-olds the right to vote, required all polling places to be accessible to the disabled in 1984, and made registering to vote easier under the National Voter Registration Act, or motor voter law, in 1993.

Ten major laws have supported this endeavor.

Improve Air Quality

Although Congress expressed its concern for clean air with passage of the 1955 Air Pollution Control Act, the law itself did little more than authorize the federal government to collect and share research on the problem. Congress provided just $5 million for the effort. When it passed the Clean Air Act in 1963, Congress moved closer toward a strong federal role but once again put most of its faith in state governments to regulate any air pollution that threatened the health or welfare of citizens.

Just two years later, however, Congress amended the Clean Air Act to give the federal government authority to set standards for automobile emissions. Although states were responsible for enforcement, the federal government was in charge of establishing a national standard that every state had to meet or beat. In 1970 Congress ordered automobile manufacturers to reduce air pollution by 90 percent, while authorizing the newly created Environmental Protection Agency (EPA) to pay states up to two-thirds of the costs arising from car inspection programs. Congress rewrote the Clean Air Act in 1990 to broaden federal authority to regulate the pollution that causes the brown haze called smog and the sulfur-heavy emissions from coal-fired electric plants that cause acid rain.

Eleven major laws have supported this endeavor.

Improve Elementary and Secondary Education

For most of American history, educating children from kindergarten through twelfth grade was the exclusive responsibility of state and local governments. That changed when the Soviet Union launched a tiny satellite called Sputnik in 1957. Fear of losing the space race led Congress to pass the 1958 National Defense Education Act, which established federal college fellowships for teacher training in math, science, and language.

Congress expanded the federal role under the sweeping 1965 Elementary and Secondary Education Act. The act set a national goal of equal access to education for every state and locality, created legal rights for poor and handicapped children, and provided $150 million in federal funding to build new schools and train teachers. Congress also enacted the 1967 Head Start program to provide preschool programs for poor children, created the Department of Education in 1979 to oversee all federal education programs, and passed the 1994 Educate America Act, which established a set of targets for educational improvement by the year 2000.

Although the federal government provides just 8 cents of every dollar spent on elementary and secondary education, it asks a great deal for its money. Under the education reforms passed in 2001, all states that accept federal funding must create testing programs for all grades.

Five major laws have supported this endeavor.

Improve Government Performance

Congress has been trying to make government more efficient since the late 1940s when it created the first of two blue-ribbon national commissions to make recommendations for reducing waste and improving performance. Many of those recommendations were implemented through reorganization plans submitted by the president and approved by Congress, creating a new organizational chart for the federal government that included the new Department of Health, Education, and Welfare, and new systems for tracking federal spending and hiring.

Congress tinkered with further reforms in the 1950s and 1960s, but returned to major reform legislation in 1978 when it enacted the Civil Service Reform Act. The federal personnel system was streamlined to make hiring and firing easier and to establish a pay-for-performance system that would reward civil servants for doing their jobs well. For most of the next two decades, Congress concentrated on improving financial management in government by assigning chief financial officers for every department and agency in 1990, creating a new government-wide performance measurement system in 1993, and streamlining the way the federal government buys everything from pencils to missiles in 1994.

Ten major laws have supported this endeavor.

Improve Mass Transportation

Ever since it provided land for the transcontinental railway system in the 1800s, Congress has been working to strengthen public transportation systems such as buses, passenger and commuter trains, and subways. In 1958 Congress passed the Transportation Act in an effort to revitalize the nation's railroads through $500 million in loans to support intercity passenger service. Twelve years later it stepped in again to rescue passenger service by creating Amtrak, the government-owned rail system that continues to lose money to this day.

Congress broadened the scope of its efforts with the 1964 Urban Mass Transportation Act, which gave cities more than $300 million to build new subways and bus systems. Although it invested another $12 billion in 1970 and provided more federal aid under the National Mass Transportation Assistance Act of 1974, Congress has been far more interested in building roads and highways than subways, light rail lines, and bus systems.

Fourteen major laws have supported this endeavor.

Improve Water Quality

Congress gave the federal government responsibility for reducing water pollution several years before it dealt with air quality. It passed

CLEVELAND PRESS COLLECTION

River on fire. Cleveland's Cuyahoga River was so polluted that it actually caught fire several times in the 1960s. Four decades later, it is now both swimmable and fishable.

the first Water Pollution Control Act in 1948, which gave states small grants to control water pollution and build sewage treatment plants. The federal government's role was strengthened under the 1965 Water Quality Act by establishing the nation's first water purity standards, which states had to meet or beat, and by creating the Water Pollution Control Administration. The law also authorized the federal government to spend $150 million on construction grants for sewage treatment facilities.

Congress continued to increase the federal government's role under the 1966 Clean Waters Restoration Act, which provided even more funding for sewage treatment, and under the 1970 Water Quality Improvement Act, which authorized the president to regulate "hazardous polluting substances" such as chemicals and other industrial by-products. Over the next twenty years, Congress expanded these laws to cover other toxic pollutants, increase federal funding, and protect marine fisheries. Under the Water Quality Act of 1987, for example, Congress ordered the federal government to protect the Chesapeake Bay and Great Lakes from further pollution and to clean up Boston Harbor.

Eleven major laws have supported this endeavor.

Increase Access to Postsecondary Education

Congress involved the federal government in helping Americans attend college long before it got involved in elementary and secondary education. Under the GI Bill, for example, Congress provided funding to allow more than 16 million World War II and Korean War veterans to attend college. It also funded the building of thousands of college classrooms, libraries, and research centers under the 1963 Higher Education Facilities Act and later established a special class of loans for students pursuing degrees in medicine or other health services. With the Middle Income Student Assistance Act of 1978 and the Higher Education Act of 1992, Congress continued to expand access to loans by raising the income limits. By 2000 all students were guaranteed access to a federally guaranteed college loan.

Thirteen major laws have supported this endeavor.

Increase Arms Control and Disarmament

Soon after development of the U.S. nuclear arsenal, Congress began trying to limit the spread of nuclear weapons. It started by ratifying the treaty establishing the International Atomic Energy Agency, which was designed to promote the development of peacetime uses of nuclear energy. Congress also created the United States Arms Control and Disarmament Agency in 1961 to advise the president on controlling the spread of weapons and ratified the 1963 Nuclear Test Ban Treaty, which prohibited the testing of nuclear devices in the atmosphere, space, territorial waters, or at sea.

Congress also ratified the 1969 Nuclear Nonproliferation Treaty, which sought to prevent the spread of nuclear technology to other nations; the Strategic Arms Limitation Treaty in 1972, which froze the number of land-based missiles and weapon-carrying submarines at then-existing levels; and the Anti-Ballistic Missile Treaty of 1972, which prohibited the United States and Soviet Union from deploying an antimissile shield. Almost twenty years later, Congress ratified the first Strategic Arms Reduction Treaty (START I), limiting the United States and Soviet Union to 6,000 nuclear warheads each.

Eight major laws have supported this endeavor.

■ Increase International Economic Development

Even before World War II had ended, Congress asked the federal government to begin strengthening the economic, civic, and educational systems of impoverished countries when it approved U.S. participation in the World Bank, an international organization that exists to this day as a source of aid to poor countries. It also approved contributions to the International Monetary Fund, another international organization that provides loans for projects that cannot attract private funding.

Congress consolidated all U.S. foreign aid into a single program under the Economic Cooperation Act in 1950, providing more than $3 billion to stimulate economic growth, and followed that with another $3.4 billion in military and economic development under the 1957 Mutual Security Act. It also approved U.S. membership in the Inter-American Development Bank, which concentrates on aid to Latin America, and expanded aid more generally under the Foreign Assistance Act of 1961. At almost the same time, Congress approved President John Kennedy's proposal for a Peace Corps of volunteers who would form "a grand and global alliance . . . to fight tyranny, poverty, disease, and war."

Eight major laws have supported this endeavor.

■ Increase Health Care Access for Low-Income Families

Congress directed the federal government to improve low-income health care access under two major laws enacted more than thirty years apart: the 1965 Medicaid Act, which allocated funds to help states provide medical assistance to the poor, and the 1997 Children's Health Insurance Program (CHIP), which funds health care coverage for poor children. Although the federal government substantially funds both programs, Medicaid and CHIP are both administered by the states as part of welfare for the needy. However, the federal government does set limits on what states can pay for with Medicaid and CHIP dollars, including a ban on the use of Medicaid money for abortions except in the case of rape, incest, or when a pregnancy threatens the life of the mother.

Two major laws have supported this endeavor.

▉ Increase Market Competition

From the late 1800s through the 1930s, the federal government created regulations in an effort to improve competition and prevent monopolies in certain industries; however, in the mid-1970s it began deregulating many of these same industries. Congress started with transportation, deregulating the airline industry in 1976, which led to the abolition of the Civil Aeronautics Board that once controlled all airline routes. Then Congress focused on the trucking and railroad industries, both of which were opened to competition in 1980. This was followed by intercity bus deregulation in 1982, which allowed bus companies such as Trailways and Greyhound to compete head-to-head wherever they wanted.

Congress also deregulated the energy industry, first by lifting price controls on "new gas" discovered after 1978 and later by eliminating controls on "old gas" discovered before 1978. Congress also deregulated financial institutions, starting in 1980 by permitting banks and savings and loan institutions to remove interest rate ceilings. Finally, Congress deregulated the telecommunications industry in 1996, opening competition in the telephone and cable television industries.

Eleven major laws have supported this endeavor.

Increase Health Care Access for Older Americans

Congress directed the federal government to help older Americans gain better access to health care under three laws: a small, but precedent-setting 1960 law that gave states federal grants to cover some of those costs; the landmark 1965 Medicare Act, which established an entirely new program to insure older Americans against medical cost; and the creation of a federal insurance program for catastrophic disease, which was repealed when older Americans rebelled against its cost.

Medicare is by far the most significant of the three laws. Passed despite intense opposition from the American Medical Association, which represents physicians, the law included two parts. The first gave older Americans insurance against hospital costs and was financed by a payroll tax on earnings. The second allowed older Americans to purchase additional insurance to cover doctor's visits, outpatient services, and laboratory bills.

Three major laws have supported this endeavor.

Increase the Stability of Financial Institutions and Markets

Congress has been protecting stock market investors since the 1933 Securities Act, which prohibited a series of practices that had contributed to the 1929 stock market collapse. In addition, Congress created deposit insurance to protect citizens from banking failures.

The federal government's regulatory role expanded with the passage of a series of laws designed to force companies to disclose more information about their finances and operations and to prevent abuse of insider information that might benefit some stock traders in the market. Under the 1964 Securities Act Amendments, for example, Congress strengthened federal oversight of stock trading and required stock exchanges such as the New York Stock Exchange to develop programs for self-policing. Congress tightened those regulations even further under the 1988 Insider Trading and Securities Fraud Enforcement Act.

During the deregulation period, however, Congress also loosened some of the rules governing the kinds of loans that savings and loan institutions could make, which in turn, eventually contributed to an industry-wide collapse. Congress then stepped in with a $50 billion bailout in 1989.

Nine major laws have supported this endeavor.

Increase the Supply of Low-Income Housing

Ever since the 1949 Housing Act, which offered federal loans to local governments for slum clearance and direct grants to create 810,000 new units of low-income housing, Congress has been developing housing for the poor and providing rent support. It authorized the federal government to continue building low-income housing under a series of laws passed in the 1960s, directed toward the needs of older Americans in 1962 and low-income families in 1965. In the latter year the Department of Housing and Urban Development was also established to help administer the growing number of housing programs.

By the late 1980s, Congress turned its attention to homelessness in general. In 1987, for example, it provided $1 billion in aid to the states to build and operate emergency shelters and food programs, create new low-income housing and apartments, and provide community health care services for the homeless.

Fourteen major laws have supported this endeavor.

Maintain Stability in the Persian Gulf

This endeavor is composed of just one major law: the congressional resolution authorizing the 1991 Gulf war against Iraq. The resolution was prompted by the Iraqi invasion of the oil-rich nation of Kuwait in August 1990. The United Nations passed its own resolution on November 29 authorizing UN forces to expel the Iraqis within sixty days. On January 12, 1991, just three days before that deadline, the Senate authorized the use of military force against

Iraq, giving the president authority to apply whatever force necessary to implement the UN resolution. On January 16 the president ordered the beginning of a month-long air war against Iraq. The House authorized the use of force the next day, and a month later the president ordered a full-scale ground assault on Iraqi forces. Exactly 100 hours later, the Gulf war ended with the Iraqi military in full retreat.

Make Government More Transparent to the Public

Starting with passage of the 1946 Administrative Procedure Act, Congress has been trying to open government to the sunshine. This law requires that all proposed rules be published in the *Federal Register*. Publication in the federal government's newspaper marks the beginning of what is known as the notice and comment period, during which those affected by the proposed regulation are encouraged to make their opinions known to the agency.

Congress also enacted the Freedom of Information Act (FOIA), signed into law on July 4, 1966, which requires that agencies open themselves up to the press and public. Using FOIA requests, citizens can ask government for information on any topic. Although the federal government always has the option to deny the request for national security purposes or to protect the privacy of other citizens, FOIA provides almost unlimited access to routine information on what government spends, how it operates, whom it employs, and what it does, as well as complete access to any information it might have on the individual citizen making the request.

A number of other laws were enacted to make government more open, including the aptly named Government in the Sunshine Act of 1975 and the Ethics in Government Act of 1978. The basic goal of all of these laws is to stop government from keeping secrets.

Ten major laws have supported this endeavor.

Promote Equal Access to Public Accommodations

Working with the federal judiciary, Congress has been striving to end discrimination in public accommodations for four decades.

Although the Supreme Court ordered the integration of the public schools in 1954, Congress pressed forward under the landmark 1964 Civil Rights Act, which prohibited discrimination based on race, religion, gender, or ethnicity across a broad spectrum of public accommodations ranging from restaurants to movie theaters to hotels. The act permitted citizens to file suit for damages in federal court against any business or individual that violated the law and allowed the Attorney General of the United States to file suit on any citizen's behalf.

Congress continued to open accommodations under the 1968 Open Housing Act, which prohibited discrimination in the sale or rental of housing, and the 1990 Americans with Disabilities Act (ADA), which required governments and private employers to make their jobs, facilities, and transportation systems accessible to the disabled. Modeled on the 1964 Civil Rights Act, the ADA lists establishments that must become accessible and includes a requirement that all public buses used on fixed routes be wheelchair accessible.

Three major laws have supported this endeavor.

Promote Financial Security in Retirement

Congress first insured older Americans against poverty under the 1935 Social Security Act, which provides income for millions of retired citizens. Under the law eligible retirees receive benefits that are weighted to deliver a greater rate of return on past payroll taxes to lower-income recipients.

Although the program was launched in the 1930s, its major expansions occurred in the 1950s, 1960s, and 1970s. In all, Congress enacted twelve separate increases in Social Security benefits from 1946 to 1972 and finally indexed benefits to rise automatically with inflation starting in 1974. Along the way Congress also created the Supplemental Security Income (SSI) program in 1971, which provides federal support for impoverished older Americans, and passed the 1974 Employee Retirement Income Security Act, which created a new federal program and agency to protect retirement pensions.

Congress also acted twice to rescue the Social Security program from funding crises. In 1977 it raised Social Security payroll taxes to compensate for a shortfall, hoping that the repair would last for seventy-five years. Just six years later, however, Congress had to pass new legislation that cut benefits, increased taxes, and raised the retirement age to avert another crisis.

Twenty-one major laws have supported this endeavor.

▓ Promote Scientific and Technological Research

With passage of the 1950 National Science Foundation Act, Congress established a federal role in both financing and exploring new technologies such as the Internet. The newly created National Science Foundation (NSF) started small with just $15 million a year, but it quickly grew into a significant source of funding for scientific, technical, and social science research.

Spurred on again by Soviet advances in technology, Congress also created the Advanced Research Projects Agency (ARPA) in 1958 as a source of intense research on military technology. Although its specific mission was military research, the agency has produced a long list of achievements of direct benefit to nonmilitary purposes, most notably generating the basic research that led to the Internet.

Four major laws have supported this endeavor.

▓ Promote Space Exploration

The Department of Defense entered the space race immediately after World War II by developing long-range ballistic missiles capable of carrying nuclear warheads. Congress expanded the effort to include the peaceful uses of space when it created the National Aeronautics and Space Administration (NASA) in 1958. Led by President Kennedy's commitment to land a man on the moon by the end of the 1960s, Congress authorized the funding for the Apollo lunar landing program.

After the last moon landing in 1972, Congress authorized development of the new Space Shuttle program, provided the dollars for deep space exploration and the Hubble telescope, and approved funds for the design, launch, and construction of an international space station. Congress also broadened NASA's ongoing research program to include high-speed computing and advanced aircraft design. Unfortunately, several of NASA's most visible post-Apollo projects ran into trouble. The Shuttle Challenger exploded just after launch in 1986, killing all seven astronauts abroad, the Hubble telescope had to be repaired because of a flaw in its huge lens, and NASA lost two Mars probes due to simple incompetence in the late 1990s.

Five major laws have supported this endeavor.

Protect Endangered Species

Congress declared that protecting endangered species was the federal government's official policy in 1966 when it gave the Department of Interior a small amount of money to acquire lands and waters for the National Wildlife Refuge System. Three years later Congress passed the Endangered Species Conservation Act, which banned the importation of any fish or wildlife on a list of endangered species. After another three years, Congress enacted the Marine Mammal Protection Act of 1972, which imposed a permanent moratorium on the killing of seals, sea lions, whales, porpoises, dolphins, sea otters, and polar bears. Congress combined these various efforts under the landmark Endangered Species Act of 1973, expanding the number of protected animals and inaugurating a program to protect species that might be threatened far into the future.

Five major laws have supported this endeavor.

Protect the Wilderness

Although Congress began setting aside parcels of land for national parks and monuments in the 1800s, it expanded the effort dramatically under the 1964 Wilderness Act. The act created an entirely new National Wilderness Preservation System to protect all national forest lands previously designated as "wilderness" or "wild," and ordered the Departments of Agriculture and Interior to inventory all federal land holdings to determine whether they should be protected from commercial use, construction of roads and recreational facilities, or mining. All totaled, the act set aside 9 million acres of wilderness for protection.

Congress ordered the federal government to protect wild and scenic rivers in 1968, including eight wild rivers such as the Shenandoah in Virginia and the Rio Grande in New Mexico, and permitted the government to purchase 100 acres of land on both sides of a protected river. Congress also passed the Surface Mining Control and Reclamation Act in 1977 to combat the adverse effects of strip mining for coal and other minerals, which involves the removal, or stripping, of all vegetation and land above a mineral deposit. It also continued to set aside more land for national parks, including 100 million acres of Alaskan wilderness in 1980 and 7.5 million acres of California desert in 1994.

Nine major laws have supported this endeavor.

■ Provide Assistance for the Working Poor

One way to prevent the need for welfare is to raise the income of poor workers, whether through tax credits, federal grants, or higher hourly minimum wages for individual workers. Congress has tried all three approaches over the past fifty years to make work more attractive than welfare. There have been eight separate increases in the minimum wage between 1946 and 1999: from 25 cents an hour in 1938, for example, to 40 cents in 1944, 75 cents in 1949, and so forth on up to $5.15 an hour by 1997.

Congress also created the Earned Income Tax Credit (EITC) in 1973, which is administered by the federal government's Internal Revenue Service. Under the EITC the working poor are eligible for federal income tax refunds each April, even if they did not earn enough money to pay any income tax at all. Congress also helped the working poor by creating the Children's Health Insurance Program in 1996.

Fifteen major laws have supported this endeavor.

Rebuild Europe after World War II

Convinced that the damage caused by World War II made the democratic nations of Western Europe more susceptible to communist takeover, Congress committed the United States to helping those nations rebuild their economies, even before peace arrived. Having approved U.S. membership in the World Bank and contributions to the International Monetary Fund, both of which promised loans to help rebuild the world economy, Congress later authorized billions in foreign aid to Europe under the 1948 Foreign Assistance Act, better known as the Marshall Plan in honor of its designer, General George C. Marshall. By the end of the program, the United States had provided $12 billion in economic aid to Great Britain, France, and its other European allies, as well as to its former enemies, Germany and Italy.

Four major laws have supported this endeavor.

Reduce Crime

Although state and local governments are responsible for the vast majority of law enforcement, Congress became increasingly concerned about fighting crime in the 1960s following widespread urban unrest, a rising crime rate, and growing worries about organized crime.

In 1968, for example, Congress provided more than $100 million to help local governments establish crime prevention programs, another $15 million for the purchase of riot control equipment, and $10 million to battle organized crime. Congress also established the first federal handgun licensing system. Two years later, it created a federal witness protection program, gave federal prosecutors new tools to detain suspects and investigate organized crime, and appropriated more money for crime control.

After years of conflict, Congress passed two laws in the early 1990s to control the sale and manufacture of guns. The first was the Brady Handgun Violence Prevention Act, which required back-

The cost of war. U.S. tanks rumble through Nuremberg, Germany, in April 1945. The United States had already begun thinking about how to rebuild Europe long before the end of the war.

ground checks on all handgun purchasers. The second was the Omnibus Crime Control and Safe Streets Act of 1994, which banned nineteen types of assault weapons; established additional federal penalties for hate crimes against victims selected for their race, religion, ethnicity, gender, disability, or sexual orientation; and required life imprisonment for criminals convicted of three federal felonies (sometimes called a "three strikes and you're out" law).

Eight major laws have supported this endeavor.

Reduce Disease

Over the past fifty years, Congress has directed the federal government to devote enormous effort to preventing and treating disease. It started in 1950 when it directed the nation's chief medical officer, the U.S. Surgeon General, to create two new public research institutes: one to study arthritis, rheumatism, and metabolic disease, and the other to study neurological diseases and blindness. Congress created a half-dozen other federal research institutes over the next fifteen years and increased federal funding for university and private research at the same time. In 1965 Congress changed its funding strategy from general medical research to more focused work on heart disease, cancer, and stroke.

In addition to research, Congress has also asked the federal government to help prevent specific diseases. It passed the 1955 Poliomyelitis Vaccine Act to combat the polio epidemic and provided additional vaccination assistance against a number of other childhood diseases in 1962. Congress also adopted a statutory ban on smoking on domestic airline flights.

Eleven major laws have supported this endeavor.

Reduce Exposure to Hazardous Waste

In 1965 Congress engaged the federal government in managing the growing volume of household and industrial waste when it passed the Solid Waste Disposal Act regulating garbage and landfills. After authorizing a two-year study of how to handle the disposal of radioactive and other hazardous wastes, the Congress enacted the landmark Resource Conservation and Recovery Act of 1976, which regulated disposal of everything from dry-cleaning fluid to toxic wastes and established the Office of Solid Waste within the Environmental Protection Agency.

Congress created the $1.6 billion Superfund program in 1980 to help the federal government clean up hazardous waste sites that have been abandoned by polluters. Although Congress gave the federal government authority to find and sue the original polluters to recover part of the cost of cleanup, Superfund was designed to begin the process well before legal action occurs.

With these solid and hazardous waste laws in place, Congress turned to the disposal of nuclear waste in 1982 and new restrictions on leaking underground gasoline tanks in 1986. Congress also required chemical manufacturers to establish right-to-know programs to alert local communities about the release of hazardous waste.

Seven major laws have supported this endeavor.

Reduce the Federal Budget Deficit

Congress has been grappling with the budget deficit ever since federal spending soared with the Vietnam War and the launch of many of the previously described social programs. Congress enacted a long list of laws over the last three decades to reduce the deficit, including the 1974 Budget and Impoundment Control Act, which created a new congressional budget process, and the 1985 Balanced Budget and Emergency Deficit Control Act, better known as the Gramm-Rudman-Hollings law, which created a never-used system of deep budget cuts as a threat against increased spending.

The budget was finally balanced after Congress and the president negotiated sweeping agreements in 1990, 1993, and 1997. The combination of spending caps, tax increases, declining defense spending with the end of the Cold War, and a booming economy produced the federal government's first budget surplus in thirty years in 1999. Unfortunately, the economic recession of 2001 drove the budget back into deficit.

Seven major laws have supported this endeavor.

Reduce Hunger and Improve Nutrition

Immediately after World War II, Congress committed the nation to reducing hunger among children when it passed the 1946 National School Lunch Act, which covers the cost of lunches for poor children. Not only did the program feed hungry children, it had the added political benefit of paying farmers and food producers for excess commodities such as cheese, pork, and milk.

Congress expanded the endeavor two decades later with two laws: the 1964 Food Stamp Act and the 1972 Special Supplemental Food Program for Women, Infants and Children (WIC). Both programs give recipients coupons that can be traded for certain foods at grocery stores and are restricted to families and women at or below certain income levels. Congress also expanded the school lunch program in 1972 by creating a summer food program for school-age children.

Five major laws have supported this endeavor.

Reduce Workplace Discrimination

For the past four decades, Congress has acted to end workplace discrimination based on race, color, religion, sex, national origin, age, or disability. The effort began with the 1963 Equal Pay Act, which required employers to provide equal pay for equal work. It continued with the landmark Civil Rights Act of 1964, which contained a specific section dealing with equal employment opportunity, to be administered by the new Equal Employment Opportunity Commission (EEOC). The law prohibited racial discrimination in the hiring process and ordered the EEOC to investigate workers' complaints about discrimination.

Congress expanded the law in 1967 to prevent age discrimination and in 1990 passed the Americans with Disabilities Act (ADA) to address discrimination against individuals with physical and mental disabilities. Under the ADA employers were ordered to make reasonable efforts to accommodate an employee's physical or mental disability. Because many complaints involve tough interpretations about what constitutes discrimination, the federal courts have played a critical role in enforcing the protections embedded in these laws.

Seven major laws have supported this endeavor.

Reform Taxes

Since the 1960s Congress has made at least two major efforts to simplify the federal government's inscrutable income tax code. The first was the 1964 Revenue Act, which overhauled the federal tax code and cut $11.4 billion in taxes for 1964 alone. The second was the 1986 Tax Reform Act, which cut rates again while collapsing fourteen different tax brackets into two. Congress also enacted a sweeping reorganization of the Internal Revenue Service in 1998 following allegations of taxpayer abuse.

Three major laws have supported this endeavor.

▓ Reform Welfare

Even as it has worked to provide a social safety net for the needy, Congress has been striving to reduce dependency on public assistance among welfare recipients. A mix of carrots and sticks has been used to encourage welfare recipients to go to work, starting with the 1981 Omnibus Reconciliation Act, which cut federal funding for a number of welfare programs, including Medicaid, Aid to Families with Dependent Children (AFDC), and Food Stamps on the theory that lower welfare benefits would drive recipients back to work. Congress tried a different approach when it passed the Family Support Act in 1988, which gave states broad authority to help welfare recipients find work through job training and job search support.

Congress passed its most significant welfare reform in 1996. Under the Personal Responsibility and Work Opportunity Reconciliation Act, Congress acted to "end welfare as we know it," as President Clinton had promised. The act put time limits on welfare benefits, required states to put at least half of all recipients to work by 2002, and cut federal welfare spending by 25 percent.

Three major laws have supported this endeavor.

▓ Stabilize Agricultural Prices

Dating back to creation of the Department of Agriculture in 1862, Congress has long supported the farming industry, but it became more aggressively involved during and after the Great Depression that devastated farmers. Congress has tried to stabilize agricultural prices through three different approaches: the purchase of agricultural surpluses such as corn and barley; direct payments to farmers to leave part of their land unplanted, thereby reducing the supply of agricultural goods; and price supports that raise the cost of commodities such as sugar.

These tactics have been employed throughout a long list of laws, including the 1985 Food Security Act, which provided $52 billion in new subsidies to address the farm crisis generated by high interest rates on land in the late 1970s and early 1980s. Another approach was taken in the 1954 Food for Peace program, which promoted agricultural exports as a way of boosting prices. Finally, in 1996 Congress completely overhauled the agriculture laws to reduce federal financial support.

Nineteen major laws have supported this endeavor.

▉ Strengthen the Nation's Airways System

Congress has long believed that states and localities are responsible for building and maintaining airports, but the federal government is responsible for creating and maintaining an integrated coast-to-coast air traffic control system. It began helping states and localities build airports under the 1946 Federal Airport Act, which provided federal funds for the construction of new airports, and began building the modern air traffic control system under the 1958 Federal Aviation Act, which created the Federal Aviation Administration (FAA).

Over the decades Congress has invested billions in airport construction and modernization, and it ordered the Civil Aeronautics Board (CAB) to regulate and allocate travel routes to the airline industry and investigate accidents. Congress transferred the latter responsibility to the National Transportation Safety Board when it was created as part of the Department of Transportation in 1966 and then subsequently abolished the CAB as part of airline deregulation.

Five major laws have supported this endeavor.

▉ Strengthen the Nation's Highway System

Congress likes nothing better than building roads and highways, if only because construction creates jobs and smooth roads back home. It committed the federal government to doing so under the 1956 Federal-Aid Highway Act, which provided funds for an initial 42,000 miles of interstate highways. Congress expanded highway aid in 1982, 1987, 1991, and 1998. Each successive bill contained more special projects in the home districts of individual members of Congress. There were just 10 projects and $262 million when Congress enacted its 1982 highway bill, 152 projects and $1.4 billion when the bill came up for its ordinary renewal in 1987, 538 projects and $6.2 billion when it came up again in 1991, and 1,850 projects and $9.3 billion when it was renewed in 1998.

Seven major laws have supported this endeavor.

Strengthen the National Defense

The United States won the cold war in 1989, in part because it committed itself to building the world's strongest defense. Congress started almost immediately after World War II by creating the modern Department of Defense in 1947, which combined the Departments of War, Navy, Army, and Air Force into a single mega-entity. Congress also invested billions in the construction of new military bases under the 1963 Defense Base Construction Act.

Having constructed a vast defense establishment, Congress soon turned to the challenge of making the Defense Department run efficiently. It reorganized the department several times during the 1970s and 1980s to promote greater efficiency and coordination. In 1983 it provided the initial funds for President Ronald Reagan's Strategic Defense Initiative, sometimes known as Star Wars, to intercept enemy ballistic missiles. With the cold war won by 1989, Congress then began to economize, starting with the 1988 Base Closure and Realignment Act, which produced a dramatic consolidation in the number of military bases around the country.

Seven major laws have supported this endeavor.

Support Veterans' Readjustment and Training

Part of building a strong defense involved helping veterans adjust to life after service. Congress began doing so in 1944 when it created the landmark GI Bill. The law provided a variety of benefits to be managed by the Veterans Administration, including home loans, education subsidies, unemployment insurance, and health and burial benefits. Congress also required employers to give veterans special preference when hiring new workers. As the number of programs, veterans' hospitals, and needy veterans grew over the years, Congress added to the benefits package. By 1987 the list of programs was so large and the veterans' lobbying groups so powerful that Congress was compelled to elevate the Veterans Administration to cabinet status.

Five major laws have supported this endeavor.

PATTERNS OF ENDEAVOR

Beyond its value as a guide to what Congress asked the federal government to do in the last half of the twentieth century, the list of endeavors offers six initial lessons about how the federal government has sought to solve the problems of the past half-century. First, many of the endeavors listed above began before World War II ended. The Food and Drug Act of 1906, the Social Security Act of 1935, and the early attempts to reserve federal lands for national parks and monuments all provided a basis for subsequent actions. Congress has also protected scientific and technological inventions for more than 200 years by providing for registration and protection of patents. These examples demonstrate that Congress rarely invents an entirely new program when it launches or expands an endeavor.

Second, despite the prevailing scholarly focus on breakthrough statutes such as Medicare or welfare reform, most of what Congress has asked the federal government to do has involved a relatively large number of statutes passed over a relatively long period of time. Only eight of the fifty endeavors involved fewer than four major statutes: devolving responsibilities to the states, enhancing workplace safety, increasing access to health care for older Americans, promoting equal access to public accommodations, reforming welfare, and reforming taxes all involved three major statutes; increasing access to health care for low-income families and maintaining stability in the Persian Gulf entailed two and one statute, respectively.

Remove these tightly focused endeavors from the list, and the average is nine statutes per endeavor. Promoting financial security in retirement involved the largest number of individual statutes, with twenty-one; followed by stabilizing agricultural price supports, with nineteen; and providing assistance to the working poor, with fifteen. Increasing the supply of low-income housing, ensuring an adequate energy supply, and improving mass transportation all entailed four-teen major statutes. Thus, almost by definition, great endeavors demand great endurance—a lesson often forgotten in the headlines about the latest legislative intrigue.

Third, many of the endeavors involve at least some effort to build or revitalize a federal agency or hire new civil servants as an instrument of implementation. Very few federal laws are self-implementing. Some require active enforcement; others require someone to write the checks, issue the food stamps, oversee the grants and contracts, or review the rules. Much as candidates and the public think government wastes too much money, they recognize that government organizations and employees are essential for sustaining an endeavor over time.

Rarely has the nation seen more striking evidence of this pattern than after the terrorist attacks on New York and Washington. Trust in the federal government to do the right thing soared in the weeks following the tragedies, as did trust in the president, vice president, the president's appointees, and federal workers. Although this "rally 'round the flag" effect had dissipated by the following spring, with the passage of time and more aggressive news reporting on the intelligence and security failures that led to the September 11 attacks, the rise confirms the role of government in reassuring Americans that life will go on after crisis.

Fourth, it is difficult to give any single president, party, or Congress the primary credit for launching and maintaining more than a handful of the endeavors. Only nine of the endeavors can be credited primarily to Democratic presidents, and just five can be credited to Republican presidents. The rest cross Democratic and Republican administrations alike. Almost by definition government's greatest endeavors reflect a stunning level of bipartisan commitment, whether reflected in repeated raises in the minimum wage or the sustained effort to contain communism. Great endeavors appear to require equally great consensus.

Fifth, several of the federal government's greatest endeavors were reactions to results of other great endeavors. Concerns about urban poverty increased as the interstate highway system spurred flight to the suburbs, increasing the income gap between inner cities and wealthier outlying areas. Pressure for welfare reform increased with worries about the dependency and potential abuse created by programs such as Food Stamps. The push for devolution intensified as the government in Washington became more involved in traditional state and local responsibilities such as crime fighting and K–12 education. And the demand for tax simplification increased as the tax code grew ever more complex with credits and loopholes designed to help various segments of the economy, be it science and technology, housing, agriculture, or defense. Thus, all fifty endeavors do not share the same vision of society.

Finally, government's greatest endeavors involved a mix of legislative strategies. Twenty-six of the fifty endeavors focused primarily on federal spending as a policy tool, including programs to provide health care to the elderly, increase homeownership, and stabilize agricultural prices. Another twenty focused primarily on regulatory strategies, including programs to improve air and water quality, end workplace discrimination, and make government more transparent to the public. The final four involved a mix of both spending and regulation. Additionally, only thirteen of the fifty involved targeted benefits for a specific group of Americans such as the elderly, poor, veterans, or racial minorities. The rest diffused benefits across society more generally. Great endeavors do not appear to require any particular strategies but do appear to thrive on wide distribution of impacts.

CONCLUSION

Congress, past presidents, and the Supreme Court have asked the federal government to aim high these past fifty years. Despite what must have seemed to be insurmountable odds at the time, the federal government attacked a host of problems that no other sector, public or nonprofit, would have or could have touched. No one knew for sure that the United States could rebuild Europe after the destruction of World War II, send a man to the moon and bring him back safely, or end racial segregation in the voting booth, housing market, and public square. But the federal government did them all. No one knew for sure that the United States could make any progress on reducing disease, building an interstate highway system, helping the economy grow, or defeating communism. But again, the federal government made progress on them all.

The federal government sustained these efforts through long periods of domestic and foreign uncertainty. If the government could make progress on its greatest endeavors after the assassination of admired leaders such as President Kennedy and Reverend Martin Luther King Jr., the urban riots of the mid-1960s, the Oklahoma City terrorist bombing in 1995, the Korean and Vietnam Wars that took the lives of 100,000 young men and women, a long list of political scandals, one presidential impeachment, and one presidential resignation, it will most certainly continue making progress in the wake of the horrific attacks of September 11, 2001.

This does not mean that all of the federal government's endeavors have been successful, however. As the next chapter shows, some endeavors have produced remarkable success, at least as measured by the perceptions of some of the nation's leading scholars of American history and political science, while others have produced dismal failure. The central concern for the next chapter is not whether government tried hard to solve a long list of problems but whether it actually succeeded in solving tough, important problems. The list of government's greatest achievements of the past fifty years is based on the answer to that question.

2

Staying the Course

Greatest Achievements of the Past Half-Century

If one mark of a great society lies in what it asks its government to do, then the mark of a great government lies in what it actually achieves. A great government does not just aim high and try hard; it also produces measurable results that build the confidence of the people it serves.

There is plenty of objective evidence that the federal government has made great progress on many of its fifty greatest endeavors of the past half-century. Europe was rebuilt after World War II and now stands as a major economic competitor to the United States; veterans of World War II, Korea, Vietnam, and the Gulf war were able to get back to their lives after service through the GI Bill; and America landed a man on the moon and brought him safely back to Earth, repeating the feat five times before the Apollo program ended in 1972. The list of objective success goes on and on:

▋ Poverty among older Americans has fallen to modern lows.
▋ The United States won the cold war.

- African American voting rates have increased with each passing election.
- Air and water quality have improved.
- The interstate highway system was built and is still expanding.
- More women are graduating from college and professional school, and more are competing in college sports.
- Food and drugs have become safer, and the drug approval process has become faster.
- More poor children are getting a head start in preschool.
- The air traffic control system was handling record amounts of traffic before September 11 and will do so again.
- More pregnant women are receiving proper medical care.
- Homeownership rates have risen to their highest levels ever.
- Americans are living longer.
- Polio and tuberculosis have been virtually eliminated.
- The Internet has revolutionized communications.
- Poor children have greater access to health care.
- Welfare rates have fallen.
- Crime rates have fallen.
- More Americans are completing high school and attending college.

Not every federal endeavor has produced success, however. Too many children still go to bed hungry, too many people are still homeless, too many workers are unable to make ends meet with minimum wage jobs, and too many citizens have too little access to health care. State and local governments still complain about the burdens of federal mandates and the lack of real devolution, Americans still wonder whether the federal government is giving enough attention to ensuring safe food and drugs, and taxpayers still get frustrated with the difficulty of obtaining reliable information from personnel at the Internal Revenue Service. Congress may have asked the federal government to aim high and try hard in solving the pressing problems of the past half-century, but it is not always clear that the federal government actually succeeded.

RATING THE ENDEAVORS

Achievement is very much in the eye of the beholder. Some Americans believe that the federal government has done enough to promote civil rights, while others believe it still has far to go; some Americans believe it has done enough to clean up the air and water, while others want to set even higher standards against pollution.

Ideally, the federal government itself would have objective measures of how well it has done in reducing poverty, improving access to higher education, protecting endangered species, and on down the list of its greatest endeavors. But such measures are extremely hard to devise and are often so narrowly focused on a specific program, such as Head Start or college loans, that one cannot infer much about the success of the overall endeavor to which each program contributes.

Absent such measures the best one can do is examine the perceptions of achievement among different groups of Americans. The general public certainly knows a great deal about government and can easily identify highly visible programs such as civil rights and the polio vaccine. It also has a broad sense about the overall contours of federal success. When asked in 1999 to think back over the entire twentieth century, Americans rated the space program as the federal government's top success and the Vietnam War as its greatest failure.[1]

Unfortunately, most Americans do not know enough about American history or public policy to rate government's fifty greatest endeavors. That task must fall to experts who know enough about the endeavors to make judgments about where the federal government achieved and failed.

This study is based on the opinions of one group of such experts: the historians and political scientists who teach at the nation's colleges and universities, specifically those who specialize in either modern American history or government. Drawn at random from the

1. Pew Research Center for the People and the Press, *Public Perspectives on the American Century: Technology Triumphs, Morality Falters* (Washington, July 1999). The full report can be found at www.people-press.org.

membership lists of the American Historical Association and American Political Science Association, roughly 1,000 academics were contacted by letter in July 2000 and asked to rate every endeavor on three measures: the importance of the problem to be solved, the difficulty of the problem to be solved, and the federal government's level of success in actually solving the problem. All totaled, 450 historians and political scientists returned the survey, producing a response rate of about 45 percent.[2] All of the ratings can be found in appendix B.

It is important to note that the 230 historians and 220 political scientists who filled out the questionnaire do not represent the American public as a whole. Most respondents had a Ph.D., roughly half had tenure at their college or university, most were white (90 percent), male (77 percent), self-identified liberals (65 percent), and Democrats (82 percent). What the final sample does represent is the American history and political science professions today, which remain mostly white, male, liberal, and Democratic. Biased though it is, this is the sample of people who are most likely to know enough about the government's past endeavors to make judgment calls on what succeeded and failed.

Degree of Importance

To the extent government is evaluated by the importance of the problems it tries to solve, the federal government aimed high over the past fifty years. Asked to rate each endeavor on a four-point scale ranging from not important (1) to very important (4), respondents gave the fifty endeavors an average rating of 3.2. The historians and political scientists did not agree on every endeavor. In statistically significant terms, men and women academics disagreed on fifteen of the fifty ratings, older and younger academics disagreed on twenty-two of fifty, historians and political scientists disagreed on twenty-one,

2. Results from the survey have a margin of error of ±5 percent, meaning that the true result among all historians and political scientists could vary by 5 percentage points in either direction of the reported answers below. The survey was administered and tabulated by Princeton Survey Research Associates.

Most Important Endeavors of the Past Half-Century

Endeavor	Percent[a]
Expand the right to vote	89
Rebuild Europe after World War II	80
Increase health care access for low-income Americans	78
Reduce workplace discrimination	78
Promote equal access to public accommodations	78
Increase arms control and disarmament	78
Improve elementary and secondary education	75
Ensure safe food and drinking water	73
Improve water quality	72
Improve air quality	72
Reduce hunger and improve nutrition	72

a. Respondents rating endeavor as very important.

conservatives and liberals disagreed on forty-two, and Republicans and Democrats disagreed on forty-one. (Unfortunately, there were simply too few minority academics in the sample to provide meaningful statistical comparisons with whites.)

The most significant differences arose among very different endeavors. Men were twice as likely as women to rate containing communism a very important problem (37 percent versus 14 percent, respectively). Academics older than sixty were more than twice as likely as academics younger than forty to say that job training was very important (39 percent versus 16 percent). Historians were almost twice as likely as political scientists to put making government more transparent in the very important category (58 percent versus 33 percent). Conservatives were roughly twenty-five times more likely than liberals to rate devolving responsibility to the states as very important (47 percent to 2 percent), and Republicans were five times more likely than Democrats to list reforming taxes as very important (57 percent to 11 percent).

The question is not whether respondents disagreed on occasion, which they did, or whether a different sample might have produced a sea change in the list of most or least important problems, which it would not. Rather, the question is whether there is any pattern in the disagreements that might shed light on how experts see the world. The answer is that the women, older academics, historians, Democrats, and liberals among the respondents tended to assign greater importance to the problems than did men, younger academics, political scientists, Republicans, and conservatives.

Thus women gave the higher importance rating to eleven of the fifteen endeavors on which they disagreed with men, older academics gave the higher rating on all twenty-two of the endeavors on which they disagreed with their younger colleagues, and historians gave the higher rating on all but five of the twenty-one endeavors on which they disagreed with political scientists. Democrats gave the higher importance rating on thirty-two of the forty-one endeavors on which they disagreed with Republicans, and liberals gave the higher rating on thirty-three of the forty-two endeavors on which they disagreed with conservatives.

There are two explanations for the pattern. First, women, older academics, and historians were more likely to be Democrats and liberal, which in turn increases their readiness to rate most problems as being more important than men, younger academics, and political scientists. This in turn increases their support for government action. This explanation fits with a time-honored pattern in American poli-

Least Important Endeavors of the Past Half-Century

Endeavor	Percent[a]
Devolve responsibilities to the states	8
Increase market competition	13
Control immigration	15
Promote space exploration	16
Reform taxes	17
Expand homeownership	18
Stabilize agricultural prices	18
Maintain stability in the Persian Gulf	24
Strengthen the national defense	28
Expand foreign markets for U.S. goods	28

a. Respondents rating endeavor as very important.

tics: one way to increase or decrease the odds of government action is to over- or underplay the size of the problem to be solved.

Second, women, older academics, and historians brought personal views, generational experiences, and academic biases that were different from their male, younger, political science colleagues. Thus men were more likely than women to rate foreign policy endeavors as very important, whereas women were more likely than men to rate reducing hunger, low-income assistance, and help for the elderly as critical goals, reflecting gender patterns found in the public as a whole. Similarly, older academics were more likely than younger academics to focus on civil rights and other 1960s-era endeavors as being more important, perhaps because so many came of political age during that era.

Degree of Difficulty

To the extent that government is also evaluated by the difficulty of the problems it tries to solve, the federal government most certainly picked its share of tough issues. Asked to rate each endeavor on a four-point scale ranging from not difficult (1) to very difficult (4), respondents gave the fifty endeavors an average rating of 2.9.

Most Difficult Endeavors of the Past Half-Century

Endeavor	Percent[a]
Advance human rights and provide humanitarian relief	66
Increase arms control and disarmament	65
Reduce workplace discrimination	53
Develop and renew impoverished communities	52
Contain communism	50
Reduce crime	48
Reduce the federal budget deficit	45
Reform welfare	43
Increase international economic development	41
Improve mass transportation	41

a. Respondents rating endeavor as very difficult.

Respondents showed far greater consensus on difficulty than on importance. In statistically significant terms, men and women academics disagreed on the difficulty of just five of the fifty endeavors (compared to eleven for importance); older and younger academics, on just seven (compared to twenty-two); and historians and political scientists, on ten (compared to twenty-one). Republicans and Democrats disagreed on the difficulty of nineteen (compared to forty-two), and conservatives and liberals disagreed on fourteen (compared to forty-one). Once again, having more women, younger academics, Republicans, and conservatives in the sample would not have altered the ranking of the most and least difficult problems.

This is not to argue that importance and difficulty are unrelated. Problems that were rated as very important tended to be rated as more difficult. The two factors are statistically significantly correlated in all fifty endeavors. It is impossible to know whether importance leads to higher ratings of difficulty or vice versa. All one can say from the analysis is that importance and difficulty are two sides of the same rating coin.

Respondents mostly agreed that some problems are easy to solve, while others are extraordinarily difficult. According to these historians and political scientists, the easiest problems to solve are the ones that involve spending money. Simply put, building highways, expanding homeownership, helping veterans, increasing access to college education, stabilizing agricultural prices, strengthening the national defense, and promoting scientific and technological research all involve little more than a commitment to bigger budgets.

Conversely, the toughest problems to solve involve efforts to alter human behavior, whether at home or abroad. It is one thing to spend more money on nutrition programs (ranked forty-first in difficulty) or increase financial security for older Americans (ranked thirty-eighth), but it is quite another to change attitudes abroad about human rights (ranked first in difficulty), eliminate the culture of dependency among welfare recipients (ranked eighth), or reduce crime (ranked sixth). That is why reducing the federal budget deficit was seen as so difficult among all groups of respondents: spending

Easiest Endeavors of the Past Half-Century

Endeavor	Percent[a]
Strengthen the nation's highway system	4
Expand homeownership	4
Support veterans' readjustment and training	6
Promote scientific and technological research	7
Increase access to postsecondary education	9
Strengthen the nation's airways system	11
Devolve responsibility to the states	11
Strengthen the national defense	11
Increase market competition	11
Reduce hunger and improve nutrition	13
Stabilize agricultural prices	13

a. Respondents rating endeavor as very difficult.

money has always been easy in the American political system, but raising taxes and cutting budgets has been extraordinarily difficult.

Degree of Success

Finally, to the extent that government is evaluated by its ability to achieve its goals, the federal government earned mostly favorable marks. Asked to rate the federal government's success in actually achieving each goal, respondents gave the fifty endeavors an average rating of 2.5 on a four-point scale from not successful (1) to very successful (4).

These percentages for success and failure suggest just how much the federal government must do to actually conquer a problem such as reducing disease, ending discrimination, or helping the needy. At least at the bottom of the list, where so few of the respondents saw government success, there is little room to mince words: government failed.

Respondents also shared a relatively high degree of consensus on success compared to importance. Men and women disagreed on the

Most Successful Endeavors of the Past Half-Century

Endeavor	Percent[a]
Rebuild Europe after World War II	82
Expand the right to vote	61
Strengthen the nation's highway system	40
Contain communism	36
Promote equal access to public accommodations	34
Reduce the federal budget deficit	33
Support veterans' readjustment and training	29
Strengthen the national defense	26
Increase health care access for older Americans	24
Promote financial security in retirement	23
Reduce disease	23

a. Respondents rating endeavor as very successful.

successfulness of ten of the fifty endeavors; older and younger academics, on seven; and historians and political scientists, on seventeen. Republicans and Democrats disagreed on the successfulness of fourteen endeavors; conservatives and liberals, on twenty.

Least Successful Endeavors of the Past Half-Century

Endeavor	Percent[a]
Increase the supply of low-income housing	0
Develop and renew impoverished communities	<1
Advance human rights and provide humanitarian relief	1
Improve mass transportation	1
Improve government performance	1
Improve elementary and secondary education	2
Expand job training and placement	2
Control immigration	3
Increase health care access for low-income families	3
Provide assistance for the working poor	3
Make government more transparent to the public	3
Reduce exposure to hazardous waste	3
Reduce crime	3
Reform welfare	3

a. Respondents rating endeavor as very successful.

Importance and difficulty had less to do with success than they had to do with each other. Whereas importance and difficulty were related on all fifty endeavors, importance and success were significantly related on only twenty-six of the fifty endeavors; difficulty and success were significantly related on just twenty of the fifty. This suggests that respondents graded each endeavor's success on its merits, not on a "curve" relative to importance or difficulty. It also suggests one last time that having more women, younger academics, conservatives, or Republicans in the sample would not have changed the top and bottom of the list significantly.

The Politics of Success

It is particularly important to note that Republicans and conservatives tended to give government higher grades on success than women, Democrats, and liberals, even though the latter three groups had given many endeavors higher ratings on importance and difficulty. Although Republicans and conservatives tended to underrate the importance and difficulty of the problems the federal government faces, they tended to overrate its success.

The reason may be simple. Academics who oppose government action tend to frame government's greatest endeavors as being simultaneously less important and difficult yet more successful, which in turn lessens the need for continuing the endeavor. Why bother to reduce workplace discrimination if the problem is not really that important or difficult and if government has already succeeded? Why bother to improve air and water quality if the problem is not particularly severe and if government has already done its job?

Democrats were almost twice as likely as Republicans to credit the government with success in reducing the deficit (35 percent versus 17 percent), while Republicans were much more likely than Democrats to say government had been very successful in ensuring safe food and drinking water (32 percent versus 12 percent). Similarly, liberals were much more likely than conservatives to say government had been very successful in building the national defense (29 percent versus 13 percent), while conservatives were much more likely than liberals to give government a very successful grade in expanding homeownership (33 percent versus 15 percent).

The ratings are linked to the notion that government has either done enough or too much in these areas. Democrats and liberals see a glass half empty on issues about which they care, while Republicans and conservatives see a glass half full. By framing these issues as less or more successful, respondents help build the case for less or more government, respectively. Just as African Americans were more likely than whites to see civil rights as one of government's greatest failures, so were historians and political scientists likely to bring their particular biases to their assessments of government's greatest hits.

Luckily, the sample shared a remarkable consensus on all but a handful of the fifty endeavors. Conservatives might have moved devolution up a few levels from the bottom on the list of importance, difficulty, and success, but not into the top ten; liberals might have moved containing communism somewhat further down in the respective ratings, but not to the bottom. As such, the ratings refute the notion that the federal government creates more problems than it solves. At least according to these experts, the federal government is fully capable of tackling important, tough problems *and* succeeding.

DEFINING ACHIEVEMENT

Even in isolation achievement is a difficult word to define. Is it just a synonym for raw success, or should it involve at least some measure of the task? Does it occur once a goal is reached, or should it require continued success over time?

Achievement is even more difficult to define when it is linked to government endeavor. Some would argue that government should only engage in endeavors that show the promise of impact. Others believe that government should reserve its energies only for important goals. Still others assert that government should concentrate its effort on important, difficult problems that no other sector can tackle.

The challenge is to rate the overall endeavor, not its separate parts. That means looking at success, importance, and difficulty. On the one hand, 20 percent of the historians and political scientists rated the space program as very successful, so that it placed thirteenth on the list of successes, while 34 percent rated it as very difficult, putting it seventeenth on the list of difficult problems to be solved. On the other hand, only 16 percent rated the space program as very important, pushing it to number 47 on the list of important problems to be solved.

Where the endeavor ranks on the list of government's greatest achievements depends entirely on how one defines the term. If achievement is a simple function of success, exploring space winds up near the top, but if it is a mix of success, importance, and difficulty, it will most certainly end up somewhere far below. The question is whether government should be rewarded for pure success regardless of the nature of the problem to be solved or given at least some credit for aiming high and trying hard.

The following list of government's greatest achievements is based on a mix of the two perspectives. It accepts the notion that success is at the core of achievement but also gives extra credit for endeavors that involve important, difficult problems. To accomplish this, 60 percent of an endeavor's final ranking is based on its successfulness, 30 percent on its importance, and 10 percent on its difficulty.

Because the list of achievements shown here and lists of failures shown in chapter 3 are based on four-point ratings of importance, difficulty, and success, it should be no surprise that academics would disagree on the final standings. Men and women disagreed on the final placement of five of the fifty endeavors; younger and older academics disagreed on seventeen; historians and political scientists, on twelve; Democrats and Republicans, on twenty-seven; and liberals and conservatives, on twenty-four.

It should also be no surprise that these disagreements reflect the same patterns found earlier. Men rated the government's achievement higher on four out of five of the disagreements; older academics, on all but two of seventeen; political scientists, on eight out of twelve; Democrats, on twenty out of twenty-seven; and liberals, on nineteen of twenty-four. Women and political scientists tended to rate government's success at lower levels than men and historians,

Government's Twenty-Five Greatest
Achievements of the Past Half-Century

Overall rank[a]	Endeavor	Ranking based on		
		Importance	Difficulty	Success
1	Rebuild Europe after World War II	2	14	1
2	Expand the right to vote	1	19	2
3	Promote equal access to public accommodations	5	12	5
4	Reduce disease	13	23	11
5	Reduce workplace discrimination	4	3	20
6	Ensure safe food and drinking water	8	36	18
7	Strengthen the nation's highway system	40	49	3
8	Increase health care access for older Americans	12	31	9
9	Reduce the federal budget deficit	34	7	6
10	Promote financial security in retirement	18	38	10
11	Improve water quality	9	21	26
12	Support veterans' readjustment and training	32	48	7
13	Promote scientific and technological research	26	47	14
14	Contain communism	38	5	4
15	Improve air quality	10	11	28
16	Enhance workplace safety	20	29	25
17	Strengthen the national defense	41	44	8
18	Reduce hunger and improve nutrition	11	41	22
19	Increase access to postsecondary education	21	46	17
20	Enhance consumer protection	22	32	23
21	Expand foreign markets for U.S. goods	42	30	16
22	Increase the stability of financial institutions and markets	35	39	21
23	Increase arms control and disarmament	6	2	35
24	Protect the wilderness	25	34	29
25	Promote space exploration	47	17	13

a. Rank is based on overall placement of each endeavor on a four-point scale running from least (1) to most (4) important, difficult, and successful.

while older academics, Democrats, and liberals tended to judge the importance and difficulty of government's endeavors at higher levels than younger academics, Republicans, and conservatives.

Adding more women, young Americans, Republicans, and conservatives to the sample of historians and political scientists that filled out this survey would have made little difference in the final rankings of government's greatest achievements and failures. As achievements, rebuilding Europe and expanding the right to vote were number 1 and 2 among all groups, while devolving responsibility to the states was number 50 among all groups except one: conservatives placed it at number 42. Having a more balanced sample of academics might have changed the rough order of endeavors ranking third through forty-seventh in achievement but not their ultimate placement at or near the top or bottom of the rankings.

LESSONS OF ACHIEVEMENT

The list of government's greatest achievements reflects some of the lessons discussed earlier regarding the patterns of endeavor. No one party, Congress, or president can be credited with any single achievement. Even Medicare, which was Lyndon Johnson's top priority in 1965, and the Marshall Plan, which was the centerpiece of Harry Truman's effort to contain communism abroad, had antecedents in preceding Congresses and administrations. Rather, achievement appears to be the direct product of endurance, consensus, and patience.

The list also underscores three other lessons of achievement. First, achievement appears to be firmly rooted in a coherent policy strategy. The government's top ten achievements center on a mostly unified regulatory or spending strategy that is anchored in a relatively clear description of the problem to be solved and is supported by enough resources, budgetary or administrative, to succeed. Interestingly, the top ten achievements also involve relatively clear and measurable results. It is easy to tell whether government is actually making progress expanding the right to vote, reducing disease, building roads and bridges, and so forth.

Second, achievement appears to reside at least partly in the moral rightness of the cause, whether a belief in human equality, a commitment to world peace and democracy, or a commitment to honor promises to previous generations. No one knew at the time whether expanding the right to vote, opening public accommodations, or ending workplace discrimination would eventually succeed. Nor did anyone have a defensible cost-benefit analysis to prove that government should act. Yet act government most certainly did, taking the moral high ground despite significant resistance.

Third, achievement reflects government's determination to intervene where the private and nonprofit sectors simply will not go. It is impossible to imagine the private sector taking the lead in rebuilding Europe or the nonprofit sector massing the capital to build the interstate highway system. In this era of promises for smaller, more limited government, it is useful to remember that the federal government appears to do best when it exercises its sovereignty to take big risks that no other actor could ever imagine taking.

These lessons are echoed in government's greatest failures. The efforts to increase the supply of low-income housing, renew poor communities, improve mass transit, reform taxes, control immigration, and devolve responsibilities to the states all have suffered from a lack of clarity regarding ends and a general reluctance regarding means. Overidentified with one party or the other, overdependent on one president or another, these endeavors were also battered by intense partisan disagreement, changing economic and social conditions, and a notable lack of public support.

A BRIEF HISTORY OF GOVERNMENT'S TWENTY-FIVE GREATEST ACHIEVEMENTS

Beneath all the statistics on importance, difficulty, and success are the stories that help explain how government actually reached its destination. The federal government largely succeeded by tackling problems and setting audacious goals that were seen as nearly insurmountable. No one knew for sure that the federal government could conquer diseases such as polio and tuberculosis, send a man to the moon and return him safely to Earth, or rebuild Europe. But the government did them all. Nor did anyone know for sure that the federal government could move families off welfare and into work, reverse two centuries of racial discrimination, or give every American a chance to go to college. But the government has made progress on all of these endeavors.

Ultimately, the essence of a great achievement can be found in the simple faith that a great society is measured in part by what it tries to do. To rephrase the great British poet Alfred Tennyson, it is better to have tried and failed than never to have tried at all.

This does not mean government should be careless when it tries to solve problems, however. It should make every effort to design programs to succeed. But there are times when government must embark on endeavors without absolute knowledge of its ultimate success. Those endeavors involve both great risk and great reward and may be the truest measure of a society's greatness. (See the Further Reading section at the end of this book for bibliographic references for the following vignettes.)

1 Rebuild Europe after World War II

The endeavor to rebuild Europe after World War II made the top of the list of government's greatest achievements the hard way: Congress asked the federal government to solve an important, tough problem, and it did just that. Nearly fifty years after the United States completed its most significant work in rebuilding Europe, this endeavor still resonates as one of the federal government's greatest achievements. The roads, railroads, bridges, and factories that had been bombed into rubble were rebuilt; the economies that had been devastated by labor shortages were rekindled; and the hunger, homelessness, and unemployment that marked the end of the war were dispatched as the war-torn continent healed.

By strengthening the economies of Western Europe, this endeavor simultaneously helped alleviate suffering abroad, contain communism, and create a vibrant market for American goods. It also

AMERICAN RED CROSS

A personal treasure. The effort to rebuild Europe involved humanitarian aid for the victims of war, including food and clothing for children. By investing in such aid, the United States strengthened support for democracy among war-weary nations.

created new economic competition that made the U.S. economy stronger and forged a bond with future allies, who subsequently fought with the United States in the Gulf war of 1991, the air war over Kosovo in 1999, and the war in Afghanistan in 2001.

This endeavor was central to the nation's broad effort to protect free people from terror and oppression. "The seeds of communism are nurtured by misery and want," President Harry S Truman argued in 1947. "They spread and grow in the evil soil of poverty and strife. They reach their full growth when the hope of a people for a better life has died." At its most basic level, rebuilding Europe involved the restoration of hope.

The endeavor itself involved several legislative initiatives at the president's request, including foreign and military aid to Turkey and Greece, two Mediterranean democratic nations considered essential in blocking communist expansion from the East, as well as the creation of a new currency system to help the world economy regain its footing. However, the centerpiece of rebuilding Europe was the 1948 Marshall Plan, named for its champion, General George C. Marshall, who had served as army chief of staff during World War II, and had just joined the Truman administration as secretary of state.

The plan itself emerged from Marshall's newly created Policy Planning Staff at the Department of State, which exists to this day and is shaping much of the diplomatic strategy surrounding the war against terrorism. Marshall's charge to his new staff was to design a program that would be accepted both abroad and at home. Their answer was outlined in a twelve-minute address Marshall delivered upon accepting a long-delayed honorary doctorate at Harvard University on June 5, 1947. Marshall wanted to announce the plan at the University of Wisconsin on May 24, but his staff could not get the outline done in time.

Marshall's announcement was anything but inspiring. Indeed, observers remember it as more of a memo-reading than an eloquent calling. Marshall toyed with his glasses, stammered here and there, and was sometimes barely audible. Nevertheless, the speech is generally considered the most important commencement address ever given at Harvard. "I need not tell you that the world situation is very serious," he started. "It is logical that the United States should do whatever it is able to do to assist in the return of normal economic health in the world, without which there can be no political stability and no assured peace. . . . Our policy is directed not against any country or doctrine but against hunger, poverty, desperation, and chaos."

Marshall had seen the poverty, hunger, and despair firsthand when he traveled through Europe in March 1947. The winter of 1946–47 had been one of the coldest in recent history, and the suffering was great. Although Marshall understood that the conditions made Western Europe ripe for civil unrest, he also embraced America's moral obligation to address the suffering across the former battlefield.

The essence of the Marshall plan was simple: inject billions in economic aid to get Europe moving again. The program, which was formally titled the European Recovery Plan, provided roughly $12 billion in aid to increase economic production, expand European trade, encourage new economic ties between former enemies, and put an end to the rampant inflation of the time.

The program was unique in two ways. First, it was limited to four years. Either it would succeed on that timetable, or it would end. Second, it demanded cooperation from the nations it was designed to help. Nations could only receive help if they created a new organization to distribute the funding. All totaled, twenty-two European nations were invited to the first planning meeting in the summer of 1947, but only sixteen showed up. The Soviet Union and its communist allies in Eastern Europe refused to attend, choosing instead to revive the Comintern, an international organization pledged to destroying world capitalism.

In retrospect, it is hard to imagine anyone being against the plan. But there was substantial opposition from Republicans and Democrats who wanted to protect U.S. workers from new competition abroad. More broadly, many Americans opposed help for Germany and Italy, particularly coming so soon after a war that had disrupted so many lives and caused so many U.S. casualties. That opposition melted away in February 1948, however, when the government of Czechoslovakia fell to the communists. Suddenly Truman's words about the seeds of communism took on clear meaning.

The Marshall Plan was adopted in the late spring of 1948 and had almost immediate success. Within two years economic production in Europe had risen 25 percent from prewar levels; within four years it was up 200 percent. West Germany experienced a particularly dramatic increase, particularly given the extent of the bombing damage inflicted during the war. By 1952 its economy was running at 1936 levels, with unemployment, homelessness, and inflation all moving downward.

By helping the United States contain communism, the Marshall Plan was a stunning foreign policy success. But it was also a great moral victory for America, prompting British Prime Minister Winston Churchill to call it "the most unsordid act in history."

The Marshall Plan continues to produce success to this day in the form of the European Economic Community (EEC), now known as the European Union, which has recently unified most of the Marshall Plan nations under a single currency (the euro) and a common, integrated trading system. This new free trade zone will help Europe compete against the United States for jobs and growth. Although some might argue that U.S. exports will suffer as a result, advocates believe that the competition is likely to make the U.S. economy more productive, which will increase economic growth at home.

As such, that $12 billion investment back in 1948 continues to yield high returns, whether measured in the new markets created by the collapse of the Soviet Union, easier movement across Europe for U.S. goods and tourists, or in the future innovations sparked by competition. The Marshall Plan also continues to provide a model for international aid and cooperation. Only days into the war in Afghanistan, U.S. Senator Joseph Lieberman (D-Conn.) proposed a new Marshall Plan for Afghanistan and the Arab world. As for the author of the Marshall Plan initiative, General Marshall became the first professional soldier to receive the Nobel Peace Prize in 1953. Although his work had done so much to help citizens abroad, he always believed that America had benefited at least as much from the effort. His plan called on the best instincts of a nation and confirmed his belief that Americans are the most generous citizens in the world.

2   Expand the Right to Vote

African American men finally won the right to vote under the Fifteenth Amendment, a simple one-sentence amendment ratified in 1870 prohibiting states from denying the right to vote on "account of race, color, or previous condition of servitude." But as if to prove that laws, Supreme Court decisions, and Constitutional amendments are sometimes ignored, states in the South quickly invented a variety of devices to raise the cost of voting for African Americans.

Some states imposed a poll tax on voters, requiring citizens to pay a fee to vote in a given election. Other states created literacy tests that required citizens to recite the constitution of the state before they would be allowed to register to vote. Still other states defined primary elections as private events, thereby evading the Fifteenth Amendment by creating a whites-only system for nominating white candidates who often ran unopposed in the general election. All of these devices worked to discourage African American participation. As of 1940 only 12 percent of African Americans were registered to vote in the South. But even if they had been registered, many would not have voted.

African American registration rates climbed to 40 percent over the next twenty years, due in part to federal pressure on a handful of southern states, and in part to the civil rights movement itself, which urged African Americans to protest a host of injustices. Voting rates also increased after the nation ratified the Twenty-Fourth Amendment in 1964, abolishing the poll tax in national elections. Unfortunately, the Twenty-Fourth Amendment did not apply to state and local elections, which meant that African Americans still faced enormous frustration converting their right to vote into reality.

All that changed after March 7, 1965, a Sunday that marked one of the bloodiest confrontations in an already bloody civil rights movement. Bloody Sunday, as it became known, began peacefully

MATT HERRON/TAKE STOCK

A registrar completes the process, 1965. The federal government sent hundreds of registrars to the South under the Voting Rights Act of 1965.

enough when roughly 600 protesters led by the Reverend Martin Luther King Jr. began walking from Selma, Alabama, toward Montgomery. King had selected Selma as the target for his voting rights campaign for obvious reasons: whereas African Americans outnumbered whites in total population, white voters outnumbered African Americans by 9,800 to 362.

The violence began only moments after the marchers crossed onto the Edmund Pettus Bridge over the Alabama River, on their way out from Selma. Acting under orders from Governor George Wallace to stop the march, state troopers waded into the crowd with tear gas, whips, police dogs, and ropes, clubbing the protesters as they knelt in prayer and eventually driving them back nearly a mile to the church where the march had begun. The next day a white

Unitarian minister from Boston was beaten to death by white men in Selma. If these events had not been televised, few Americans would have believed the brutality.

Calling Bloody Sunday "an American tragedy," President Lyndon Johnson convened a special session of Congress on March 15 to demand immediate action on voting rights. It was one of his greatest speeches ever. Standing before a joint session of Congress, Johnson compared Selma to Appomattox as a place where "history and fate" had met to "shape a turning point in man's unending march for freedom." After first reminding Congress that "it is wrong—deadly wrong—to deny any of your fellow Americans the right to vote in this country," Johnson declared that "we have already waited a hundred years or more, and the time for waiting is gone. Their cause must be our cause too, because . . . really it is all of us, who must overcome the crippling legacy of bigotry and injustice. And 'we shall overcome.' " His oration was almost as moving as King's "I have a dream" speech two years before and is said to have moved King to tears.

Bloody Sunday not only propelled the Voting Rights Act to passage within five months, it made the bill much tougher than it otherwise would have been. The final law included seven separate sections that guarantee voting rights to this day, including one giving the federal Department of Justice the authority to dispatch federal examiners to register citizens to vote in the seven states fully covered by the law—Alabama, Georgia, Louisiana, Mississippi, South Carolina, Virginia, and twenty-six counties in North Carolina—as well as in one county in Arizona. Although South Carolina immediately challenged the law as a violation of its constitutional obligation to determine the times, places, and manner of elections, the Supreme Court voted 8-1 to reject the argument.

The law began to work its will almost immediately. Within a year federal registrars had added 124,000 African Americans to the voting rolls. By the end of 1966, they had added nearly a million more.

As its successes mounted in the South, Congress expanded the Voting Rights Act to the rest of the nation. In 1970, for example,

Congress extended the ban on literacy tests to cover all fifty states and established a thirty-day residency requirement in all presidential elections, thereby reducing the use of long lead times for registration as a device for preventing participation. These changes added another 1.5 million African Americans to the registration rolls, as well as hundreds of thousands of other minority voters.

With new voters going to the polling place in record proportions, the number of African American elected officials began to rise. Between 1970 and 1988, for example, the number of African American state legislators in the eleven former states of the Confederacy increased from 40 to 192.

Congress did not restrict this endeavor only to African Americans, however. With eighteen- to twenty-one-year-olds dying on the field of battle in Vietnam, Congress decided to allow Americans in this age group to vote in federal elections at home. Faced with the prospect of running two election systems, one for federal elections that allowed younger Americans to vote and another for state and local elections that did not, states ratified the Twenty-Sixth Amendment in 1971, giving young Americans the right to vote in all elections. Under the 1993 National Voter Registration Act, which is often called the motor voter law, states must allow citizens to register whenever they get other state and local services such as a driver's license (hence the term *motor voter*) or a welfare check.

According to early estimates, nearly 45 million new voters had registered under the law by 2000. Although most of the new voters registered at driver's license bureaus, 10 to 20 percent signed up at public welfare agencies. By reducing the costs of registering for poor Americans, the motor voter law helps reduce some of the bias in the current registration system. Contrary to early expectations that most of these new voters would register as Democrats, neither party has benefited from the easier registration.

However, the 2000 election showed that expanding voting rights must be a continuing endeavor. It is not enough merely to get all Americans registered to vote and not even enough to get registered voters to cast ballots on election day. The 2000 election proved that protecting voting rights also involves making sure that every vote counts. No matter what one believes about who actually won the Florida vote, be it George W. Bush or Al Gore, many citizens lost their right to vote by using antiquated, poorly maintained voting machines. Until every voter has access to decent technology and easily understood ballots, this endeavor will remain a work in progress.

3   Promote Equal Access to Public Accommodations

Like the right to vote, the campaign to open public accommodations to all Americans involved decades of struggle. The effort was not over when the nation ratified the Thirteenth Amendment abolishing all forms of slavery in the United States. Important though the amendment was in ending slavery, it did not give the former slaves any protection from discrimination as free men and women, and it did not stop states from enacting so-called black codes, which prohibited African Americans from owning property, making contracts, and otherwise restricting the free movement of former slaves.

Nor was it over when Congress enacted the Civil Rights Acts of 1866, 1867, 1870, 1871, or 1875, which gave citizens "of every race and color" the same right to make and enforce contracts, sue and be sued, participate in politics, vote, and be given "the full and equal enjoyment" of public accommodations such as hotels, transportation, or theaters.

Nor was it even over when the nation ratified the Fourteenth Amendment in 1868. The intent of the amendment is unmistakable in its second sentence: "No state shall make or enforce any law which shall abridge the privileges or immunities of citizens of the United States; nor shall any State deprive any person of life, liberty, or property, without due process of law; nor deny to any person within its jurisdiction the equal protection of the laws."

As if to prove again that laws and constitutional amendments can be broken, racial discrimination continued well into the 1900s, fueled in part by Supreme Court decisions that upheld the "Jim Crow" laws that many states had passed to classify and segregate Americans by race. Even as African Americans formed new organizations such as the National Association for the Advancement of

Segregation in public accommodations, circa 1950. The Civil Rights Act of 1964 put an end to "separate, but equal" treatment in the nation's public accommodations, including bus stations, restaurants, and hotels.

Colored People (NAACP) to continue fighting those laws in the courts, they also began demanding change through a social movement around civil disobedience and boycotts.

It was an act of civil disobedience, for example, that created the successful Montgomery, Alabama, bus boycott in 1955. African Americans stopped riding the city buses after a seamstress and local NAACP member, Rosa Parks, was arrested for violating the city's Jim Crow law by refusing to move to give up her seat on a city bus to a white citizen. The boycott ended 381 very long days later when the Supreme Court ruled that bus segregation was unconstitutional. The boycott not only proved the economic power of African Americans, it gave a young minister named Martin Luther King Jr. his first national victory as a civil rights leader.

By then African Americans also had won a major victory in the Supreme Court's 1954 decision in *Brown* v. *Topeka Board of Education*, a case that shows just how important the federal judiciary is to many of the federal government's greatest endeavors. The case involved a simple request from an eight-year-old child named Linda Brown who merely wanted to go to a public school just down the street. When the local school board said no, Brown and her parents appealed all the way to the Supreme Court. With help from NAACP lawyers once again, the case forced the nation to ask how such a tiny girl could generate so much hate.

Brown was actually a blend of five school desegregation cases (from Delaware, Kansas, South Carolina, and Virginia) and was examined after a three-year wait on the Supreme Court docket. Knowing that the order to integrate the public schools would provoke intense opposition in the South, the Supreme Court decided to wait until after the 1952 election to issue its landmark decision, splitting the case in two. In the end *Brown I* asked whether a child could get an equal education in a separate but equal setting. As opposed to earlier decisions, the Supreme Court unanimously answered no, declaring that separate educational facilities are "inherently unequal." Using the Fourteenth Amendment's promise of equal protection of the laws as the basis for its ruling, *Brown I* concluded that Linda Brown had been denied equal protection under the Fourteenth Amendment, and *Brown II* ordered the states to desegregate their schools "with all deliberate speed."

Even as the *Brown* cases swept away hundreds of laws, they provoked intense opposition from the South. Many southern politicians vowed to block schoolhouse doors, and southern states encouraged their school districts not to comply with the Supreme Court's order. The governor of Arkansas even put 270 state troopers around Little Rock's Central High School in the fall of 1957 to prevent just nine African American students from entering the building. Although the governor backed down when President Dwight Eisenhower ordered federal paratroopers into Little Rock, the endeavor was still not strong enough to succeed.

The movement to break down the color barrier reached a crescendo in the summer of 1963 with a massive march on Washington and a powerful speech from King. Addressing 250,000 demonstrators gathered at the Lincoln Memorial, King gave one of the most moving political speeches in American history, part of which read:

> I have a dream that one day on the red hills of Georgia, the sons of former slaves and the sons of former slave owners will be able to sit down together at the table of brotherhood. I have a dream that one day even the state of Mississippi, a desert state sweltering with the heat of injustice and oppression, will be transformed into an oasis of freedom and justice. I have a dream that my four little children will one day live in a nation where they will not be judged by the color of their skin but by the content of their character.

King's speech had a dramatic effect on public opinion but not on Congress. Although he won the Nobel Peace Prize in 1964 for his work, congressional opponents easily derailed a new civil rights bill by merely threatening to talk the bill to death through a Senate filibuster that can only be broken by a sixty-vote majority. By the end of 1963, the civil rights movement was stalled as the nation mourned the assassination of President John F. Kennedy and wondered how Johnson would govern.

Johnson quickly answered by demanding immediate legislative action on Kennedy's civil rights agenda. As a former schoolteacher from Texas, Johnson knew firsthand how racism and poverty could devastate communities; as a former Senate majority leader, he knew how to break a filibuster. By defining civil rights as a way to honor the fallen president, Johnson rallied public opinion to the effort, breaking the southern opposition after a brutal two-and-a-half-month filibuster.

With the opposition exhausted, the Senate finally passed the Civil Rights Act of 1964 in June. Like the civil rights acts of the 1860s and 1870s, the 1964 act prohibited a range of practices that were part of the black codes established after the Civil War. But unlike the acts of old, which did not carry strong federal penalties for failure to obey, the 1964 act authorized the U.S. attorney general to withhold federal funds from any government program that was not desegregated and to bring lawsuits in federal courts to force action while giving citizens the right to appeal certain kinds of discrimination to the new Equal Employment Opportunity Commission (EEOC).

It is safe to say that the Civil Rights Act was the single most important step toward ending segregation in the United States. At the core of the act was an outright prohibition against discrimination on the basis of race, color, sex, religion, or national origin, whether by employers or labor unions in businesses (Title VII) or in hotels, restaurants, theaters, gas stations, and all other public accommodations that affect interstate commerce, as well as in any and all public facilities (Title II). The act also provided federal grants to help states integrate the public schools (Title IV), allowed the federal government to withhold federal funds from public or private programs such as colleges and universities in which discrimination is allowed to occur (Title VI), and authorized the Equal Employment Opportunity Commission to receive and adjudicate complaints based on Title VII.

Once again, the effort to expand civil rights involved more than African Americans and more than amendments to the Civil Rights Act. It has also involved other laws that have copied the Civil Rights Act's enforcement mechanisms to protect Americans in a host of settings. Under Title IX of the 1972 Education Amendments, which was enacted by a Democratic Congress and signed into law by a Republican president, the federal government and its Department of Health, Education, and Welfare (which was divided into the Departments of Education and of Heath and Human Services in 1978) were given the power to prohibit gender discrimination in any institution that receives federal education funds, meaning almost every institution of learning in the nation.

Faced with a choice between giving women equal opportunity to advance or losing federal dollars, the vast majority of institutions did the right thing and encouraged more women to enroll and graduate, thereby closing the gender gap in college education. In 1971 before Title IX, only 18 percent of female high school graduates had completed four years of college, compared to 26 percent of males. By its twenty-fifth anniversary in 1996, 27 percent of both sexes had completed four years of college.

Although Title IX has affected all levels of American education and all walks on campus, its most visible impacts can be seen on the athletic fields. Before Title IX an estimated 50,000 men attended college on athletic scholarships compared to just 50 women. By the year 2000, college women received roughly a third of all athletic scholarships in everything from ice hockey to wrestling to rugby. This increase has drawn more girls to middle school and high school sports and increased the visibility of women's athletics at the Olympic and professional levels. "Without Title IX, I'd be nowhere," says Cheryl Miller, a member of the U.S. basketball team that won the 1984 Olympic gold medal.

The true impact of Title IX is not in Olympic glory, however. Rather, it is in the small steps taken in classrooms that were once largely closed to women. Between 1972 and 1992, for example, the number of female business majors increased from 8 percent to 47 percent, while the number of female biology majors jumped from 28 percent to 52 percent. Even as the nation rightly celebrates the accomplishments of women on playing fields, equally dramatic accolades are being won in academic fields where women were once deemed ineligible to compete.

4 Reducing Disease

Protecting the nation from foreign and domestic threats involves more than fighting wars and enforcing laws. It also involves protecting Americans from hidden threats such as disease, pollution, and unsafe foods. As science has learned more about preventing disease, the federal government's role has grown, whether through funding for advanced scientific research or programs to make sure all Americans are vaccinated against life-threatening illnesses.

Although they did not address health and safety directly, the Founders would certainly embrace the notion of vaccinating children against deadly diseases. Federal involvement in buying and distributing vaccines has saved countless lives and billions of dollars spent on the costs of treating preventable diseases.

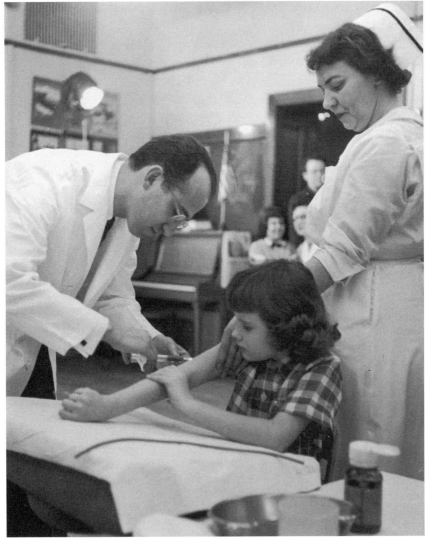

REUTERS/STR/ARCHIVE PHOTOS

Preventing disease. Dr. Jonas Salk, inventor of the polio vaccine, demonstrates his technique. The vaccine, distributed under the Polio Vaccination Act, stopped the epidemic of the devastating disease.

The federal role in vaccinating children against life-threatening illnesses dates back to the very beginning of the vaccination era in the 1940s and 1950s. Congress passed the Poliomyelitis Vaccination Assistance Act in 1955 to cover the cost of free vaccines against the deadly, crippling childhood disease and added the Vaccination Assistance Act in 1961 to help state governments immunize all children against polio, diphtheria, whooping cough, and tetanus by the age of five.

The Polio Vaccine Act, for short, was a desperately needed act for a desperate time. Americans were not quite sure how, when, or why the highly contagious poliovirus was transmitted. Epidemics seemed to rise with the summer heat, leading parents to ban their children from swimming pools, parks, and playgrounds during the summer. And once the virus was caught, it seemed unstoppable. Some victims were permanently paralyzed; others were condemned to live in iron lung machines the size of a compact car that helped them breathe. Still others were strapped into leg braces to help them walk.

President Franklin D. Roosevelt had been stricken by polio as an adult but hid his dependence on a wheelchair and braces throughout his four-term presidency. He traveled to Warm Springs, Georgia, for treatment every summer and created a private foundation in 1938, now known as the March of Dimes, to conduct research on the disease.

Ironically, the virus became more dangerous as a result of vast improvements in the public health system, including safer drinking water and better sanitation systems. Protected from early exposure to less-damaging forms of the virus, children grew up without immunity to far more threatening strains. Although the disease was never as widespread as smallpox, its crippling effects were so terrifying, its victims often so young, and its causes so unclear, that its spread created widespread panic. Fear led to quarantines; quarantines led to greater fear.

The federal government became involved in the crisis in 1955 when Jonas Salk finally developed a vaccine against the virus. Suddenly the nation knew how to prevent the disease; it just did not know how to make sure every child was protected. That is where the federal government came in. Under the 1955 Polio Vaccine Act, Congress provided the funding to make sure every child in the country received the vaccine. Congress also required the federal government's chief health officer, the Surgeon General, to set standards for the testing and distribution of the vaccine to millions of children, without regard to their families' ability to pay.

The federal government continues to promote vaccination against childhood diseases through the National Immunization Program at the Centers for Disease Control (CDC). The CDC was created by Congress in 1946 and remains headquartered in Atlanta, Georgia, where its predecessor, the Communicable Disease Center, had been located for proximity to the mosquito-spread malaria that it was originally created to fight.

Designed to help states and localities educate parents about the need for vaccinations and monitor the supply of vaccines, the immunization program has been a remarkable success. Since the 1950s when the federal government began distributing vaccines, the incidence of most childhood diseases has fallen by 95 percent or more. The number of polio cases dropped from 15,000 a year in the 1950s to zero today, while German measles has virtually disappeared from the Western Hemisphere.

The program has also produced a stunning return on investment. Every dollar spent immunizing children against measles, mumps, and rubella saves $21 in future health costs, for example, while every dollar spent on vaccinations for diphtheria-pertussis-tetanus saves $29.

The CDC and its 7,800 employees do more than operate the national vaccination program, however. They also conduct deep research on some of the nation's most troubling health issues, which has led to significant reductions in heart disease and significant gains in cancer survival rates. The CDC's disease detectives have been at the forefront of identifying a host of mystery illnesses, including the respiratory disease that attacked attendees at an American Legion convention in 1968 (Legionnaire's disease), toxic shock syndrome in 1980, and hepatitis C in 1989, while tracking down the causes of major health disasters, including the outbreak of food poisoning at

Jack in the Box hamburger outlets in Washington state in 1993 and the emergence of a new strain of flu in 1997.

The CDC has a role in homeland defense by preparing the nation for a possible biological attack. That means preparing stockpiles of vaccines and pharmaceuticals that can be delivered to any site within twelve hours of an incident, monitoring disease outbreaks through a "sentinel" system that involves emergency rooms and infectious disease specialists across the country, and issuing guidelines on everything from handling the mail to diagnosing a new form of biological or chemical attack. In late November 2001, the CDC purchased 155 million doses of smallpox vaccine to make sure the nation was protected against this deadly form of biological terrorism.

The CDC is not the only federal agency involved in reducing disease nor even the oldest. That honor belongs to the National Institutes of Health (NIH), which date back to 1887 when the federal government opened a one-room laboratory on Staten Island, New York, to study infectious diseases carried to the United States on passenger and cargo ships.

As the inventory of infectious diseases grew, so did the federal government's involvement in health care research. Congress established the National Institute of Health (singular) in 1930, added the National Cancer Institute in 1937, and created a division of research grants to promote outside (or extramural) research in 1946. New institutes for dental research, experimental biology, health disease, mental health, and microbiology were created in 1948, accompanied by a change in the NIH's middle name to the plural "Institutes." Subsequently, Congress expanded the research budget from a mere $4 million in 1947 to $100 million in 1957, created the National Institute of Allergy and Infectious Diseases in 1955, added two new institutes in 1962 for Child Health and Human Development and for General Medical Sciences, and created a National Institute on Aging in 1974. And it has continued to add: by 2001 the NIH had twenty-seven separate institutes housed in its seventy-five buildings on a 300-acre campus in Bethesda, Maryland.

This investment has made a dramatic difference in the quality of life for most Americans. Deaths from heart disease are down by more than a third since the mid-1970s, five-year cancer survival rates are up by 60 percent, schizophrenia and depression are much more treatable, and dental sealants now prevent virtually 100 percent of cavities in children. Although there are still significant differences in disease rates between the rich and poor and among African Americans, Native Americans, and whites, Americans in general are living longer, healthier lives because of the federal effort to reduce disease.

This investment has also created a new wave of challenges in covering the costs of an aging society, including the increasing cost of Medicare and Social Security. In 1900 only one of every twenty-five Americans was over the age of sixty-five. By 1950 the number was one in twelve, and by 1985, one in nine. By 2030 it will be one in five. In 1900 the average American lived to age forty-seven; by the year 2000, the average had increased to seventy-nine; by the year 2030, the number will be in the mid-eighties. No one knows yet whether the Rolling Stones and the Eagles will still be winning Grammys, but their fans will still be alive and active.

The increase in life span is largely due to a decline in death at early ages. More children are surviving childhood as vaccinations and better nutrition and sanitation now prevent many of the illnesses that killed so many children in previous generations. More of today's middle-aged Americans will live to retirement age as medical research renders once-deadly diseases such as diabetes and asthma manageable. And more sixty-five-year-olds will live into their eighties, benefiting from improved survival rates for heart attacks and cancer, as well as from the effects of preventive medicine earlier in life.

The fact that more Americans now survive the early and middle years of life ensures that more will live past their seventies and eighties. Indeed, the number of "oldest old"—defined as people over age eighty-five—is expected to grow from just over 3 million today to almost 17 million by 2050, and over the same time period, the number of people over 100 is expected to jump from 45,000 to over 1 million. By 2040 when the baby boomers are fully retired, nearly one-fourth of the entire U.S. population will be over the age of sixty-two, while one in nine Americans will be over the age of seventy-five.

5 Reduce Workplace Discrimination

The United States has one of the most diverse work forces in the world. There have never been more women, African Americans, Hispanics, Asian Americans, or disabled Americans in the workplace. Only 15 percent of new workers are white males, compared to almost 50 percent in the early 1980s.

As employee diversity has grown, so have calls for expanded protection against workplace discrimination. Many of the disputes have been settled in the Supreme Court, where women, older Americans, and the disabled have won a series of victories using the 1964 Civil Rights Act, the 1967 Age Discrimination Act, and the 1990 Americans with Disabilities Act to advance their cause. Again, laws are not self-implementing. They must be enforced, whether by presidents, federal agencies, or the courts.

For these Americans the effort to reduce workplace discrimination is one of the most recent endeavors on the list of government's greatest achievements. For most of American history, for example, the federal government sheltered women from what it saw as the harsh realities of the workplace. In *Muller* v. *Oregon* (1908), for example, the Supreme Court upheld an Oregon law limiting the number of hours women could work in factories by making a simple determination: "The two sexes differ in the structure of the body, in the functions to be performed by each, in the amount of physical strength, in the capacity for long-continued labor, particularly when done standing."

Having been frustrated for well over a century in the campaign to limit sex discrimination, the women's rights movement won its greatest victory when Congress added the word "sex" to the prohibition against discrimination on the basis of "race, color, religion, or national origin" in the 1964 Civil Rights Act. Ironically, it was a conservative Virginia Democrat, Howard W. Smith, who offered the amendment adding women to the bill, believing that his colleagues would never vote for a bill guaranteeing equality of the sexes. Once the bill passed, women had the legislative lever they needed to

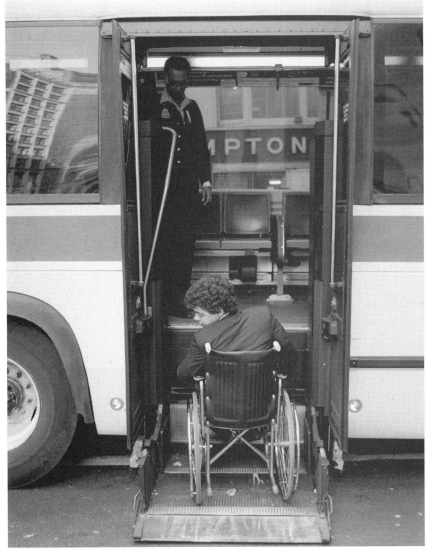

©BETTMANN/CORBIS

A kneeling bus. Under the Americans with Disabilities Act, state and local bus systems had to make their transportation systems wheelchair accessible.

demand workplace protection. However, they needed help from the Supreme Court to make sure the laws were interpreted and enforced.

Many of the most important cases came in the 1980s and 1990s. In 1986, for example, the Supreme Court ruled that merely having a formal policy against sexual harassment did not excuse a company from its responsibility to create a climate free of "intimidation, ridicule, and insult." In 1987 the Supreme Court upheld a California law that required companies to provide unpaid maternity leave for women.

The Supreme Court continued to expand protections for women in the workplace in the 1990s, issuing a series of rulings that held employers responsible for discrimination and harassment by their employees. In *Harris* v. *Forklift Systems* (1993), for example, the Supreme Court declared that women need not prove psychological harm or an inability to do their job to win a judgment of sexual harassment. As Justice Sandra Day O'Connor wrote for the unanimous Court: "A discriminatory abusive work environment, even one that does not seriously affect employees' psychological well-being, can and often will detract from employees' job performance, discourage employees from remaining on the job, or keep them from advancing in their careers." In *Faragher* v. *City of Boca Raton* (1998), a 7-2 majority agreed that employers, not just individual employees, are responsible for preventing sexual harassment in the workplace. Even if they do not know that a supervisor is harassing an employee, employers can be held liable for damages.

Despite these decisions, women still trail men on arguably the most important measure of workplace equity: pay. Although the 1963 Equal Pay Act requires that men and women be paid equal pay for similar work, much of the current pay gap is due to the concentration of women in lower-paid occupations. This de facto discrimination has led the women's movement to argue for laws that require equal pay for *comparable* work, meaning work that is worth the same to an employer even if it involves very different *tasks* and skills.

Just as African Americans were not the only citizens to be protected from discrimination in public accommodations, women were not the only citizens to be protected from workplace discrimination.

Although the federal government has been working to ensure access to public transportation for disabled Americans for thirty years, it was not asked to protect disabled Americans from workplace discrimination until Congress passed the landmark Americans with Disabilities Act (ADA) in 1990.

Led in part by then-Senate minority leader and future Republican presidential nominee Robert Dole, who lost the use of his right arm in World War II, Congress extended civil rights protection to individuals with either a physical or mental impairment that limits one or more of a list of "life activities" such as being able to dress or feed oneself. As of 1990 more than 20 million Americans qualified for protection under the ADA, including more than 13 million who had impaired eyesight or hearing, 8 million who had difficulty walking, and 1.3 million-plus who were confined to wheelchairs.

Under the ADA all public accommodations, meaning hotels, restaurants, buses, theaters, and sports stadiums, must be accessible to people with disabilities. Employers may not discriminate against qualified people with disabilities in hiring, advancement, pay, or training, and must adjust the workplace to accommodate them if necessary, even if that requires new application procedures, more access, even special computers. In addition, all new buses, trains, and subway cars must be wheelchair accessible, and all telephone companies must provide relay services allowing people with voice or hearing impairments to place and receive calls from ordinary telephones.

Once again, however, passing a law is only the first step toward achievement. Complaints must be filed, cases won, court orders enforced, public opinion changed. Moreover, compliance with the ADA is so costly that some firms have refused to follow the law until they are sued.

By 1998 the first two ADA lawsuits reached the Supreme Court. In *Bragdon* v. *Abbott*, a 5-4 majority agreed that the law's definition of disability applied to people infected with the HIV virus that causes AIDS, even when there is no evidence of the disease. And in *Pennsylvania Department of Corrections* v. *Yeskey*, which was also decided in 1998, a unanimous Supreme Court ruled that the ADA applied to state prison inmates, who could not be segregated from other prisoners on the basis of disability. The effort to reduce workplace discrimination demonstrates the importance of both law and enforcement in creating government achievement. Unlike rebuilding Europe and reducing disease, where progress was made through bricks and mortar, much of the progress in expanding voting rights, opening public accommodations, and attacking workplace discrimination involved a combination of legislation and judicial action. Congress can pass all the laws it wants, but it must rely on the federal courts to make those laws stick. Similarly, the courts can make all the decisions they wish but need Congress, the president, and the federal bureaucracy to make those judgments real.

6 Ensure Safe Food and Drinking Water

The federal government has been working to protect citizens from tainted food and unsafe drinking water since 1906 when Congress passed the Food and Drug Act and the Federal Meat Inspection Act. Stunned by publication of *The Jungle*, Upton Sinclair's muckraking book about the meat packing industry, Congress prohibited interstate commerce in misbranded food and drugs, which in turn gave the federal government authority to demand truth in labeling and inspect food processing plants. Congress also created a new program within the Agriculture Department to inspect all cattle, sheep, pigs, goats, and even horses at the slaughterhouse.

These two laws provided the platform for repeated expansions over the years. The Agriculture Department added the poultry industry to its inspection list in the 1920s, and Congress expanded the effort under the 1957 Poultry Products Protection Act. Congress also rewrote the Food and Drug Act in 1938 to give the Food and Drug Administration (FDA) new powers to make sure that food and drugs were not only properly labeled but safe to eat and use, then expanded it again and again over the years to keep pace with scientific breakthroughs and new threats to public safety, including bioterrorism.

Congress added a new law to the inventory in 1947 when it passed the Federal Insecticide, Fungicide and Rodenticide Act,

Looking for danger. A Centers for Disease Control specialist takes a water sample from a spring suspected of harboring *E. coli* bacteria.

requiring the labels of all pesticides to be registered with the Agriculture Department before being sold. It returned to the meat inspection effort in 1967 when it gave the federal government the power to set uniform standards for all of the nation's 17,000 slaughterhouses and packing plants, of which only 2,000 had been covered under the 1906 act. "Nobody in this country ought to ever take a chance on eating filthy meat from filthy packing houses," Johnson said in signing the bill, "it doesn't make any difference how powerful the meat lobby is."

Public demand for protection swelled in the 1960s, in part due to the publication of Rachel Carson's *Silent Spring*, which heightened public worries about pesticides, and the creation of environmental interest groups such as Ralph Nader's Public Citizen, the Natural Resources Defense Council, and Greenpeace that joined forces with existing organizations such as the Nature Conservancy (1951), the Wilderness Society (1935), and the Sierra Club (1893). Between 1965 and 2000, Congress passed a long list of laws to protect citizens from environmental harm. Safe food and water were swept along in the same movement that brought new protections against hazardous waste, asbestos, leaking underground storage tanks, garbage, indoor radon, and lead contamination.

Having a Congress controlled by one party and the presidency controlled by the other is often characterized as the worst possible circumstance for passing legislation. Although divided government, as such situations are called, makes legislative passage more difficult, Congress has passed some of the nation's most important legislation during just such periods, including many of the laws listed above.

The Safe Drinking Water Act is a nearly perfect example of bipartisan lawmaking. Driven by concerns about the relationship between impure drinking water and cancer in New Orleans and Pittsburgh, the act gave the federal government its first authority ever to regulate drinking water contaminants suspected of causing chemical poisoning or cancer. The first version of the statute was passed by voice vote in 1974 by a Democratic Congress and signed into law by a Republican president; the first set of amendments was passed in 1986 by a Republican Congress and a different Republican president; and a third and final set of amendments was passed in 1996 by a Republican Congress and a Democratic president. The Safe Drinking Water Act has been a success almost entirely because of legislative actions by divided government.

The act itself established national drinking water standards for any system serving at least twenty-five people or fifteen homes, meaning roughly 80 percent of the American public and 250,000 drinking water systems. Administered by the Environmental Protection Agency (EPA), itself created in 1970, the act also gave the federal government the authority to regulate a number of threats to water purity, including bacteria, nitrates, metals, lead and copper, and radioactive nuclides, all of which endanger human health. Congress gave the EPA additional authority to regulate water quality under 1986 amendments to the Drinking Water Act, which led to rules governing more than eighty drinking water contaminants. Congress also transferred responsibility for regulating pesticides from the farmer-friendly Agriculture Department to the EPA in 1974, giving the newly created Office of Ground Water and Drinking Water the power to regulate all threats to water purity.

The Safe Drinking Water Act involved more than regulation, however. It also created a public notification system to alert citizens to water system violations and gave the EPA authority to protect underground sources of drinking water. Because many states and localities cannot improve water quality without investing in new technologies and treatment facilities, Congress also gave the EPA authority in 1996 to create a nearly $3 billion loan fund to help those governments pay the cost. But even as they build the new systems, the EPA must keep up with new contaminants while making sure that the standards it has already set are neither too low for public health nor too high to be implemented.

Ensuring safe food and drinking water is likely to be a federal endeavor far into the future, whether because of new threats to food safety such as "mad cow disease" or because of pressure from the public for higher water quality standards on contaminants such as arsenic. Moreover, merely keeping up with population growth imposes substantial pressure on the federal government's public health agencies. A great number of Americans still drink from contaminated wells and aquifers, packing plants still have problems with cleanliness and bacteria, and advertisers often overstate the health benefits of nutritional supplements, vitamins, and even teas.

7 Strengthen the Nation's Highway System

The U.S. government entered the road-building business long before the Founders went to Philadelphia to write a new constitution. In fact, it became involved in building roads even before the Declaration of Independence was signed, when the first Continental Congress appointed Benjamin Franklin as the nation's first post-master general. Delivering the mail meant building the roads, which the young nation did mile by painstaking mile.

Building roads was about more than just moving the mail, however. Roads were a way to build the economy by encouraging interstate commerce and a way to build national identity by linking communities to a greater whole.

Even with airplanes and e-mail, roads are still an essential part of connecting states to states and communities to communities, which is why the national government is still adding to the nearly 43,000 miles it has built as part of the interstate highway system. Although the interstate highway system represents just 1 percent of all highways in the country, it carries nearly one quarter of all roadway traffic and more than sixty times as much traffic as all passenger rail services. It may not be as charming as the old two-lane U.S. highway system it replaced, but it is much safer. According to estimates from the Federal Highway Administration, use of the system may have saved 200,000 lives since the first mile of pavement was laid in 1957.

The system did not come cheap. Established by Congress under the Interstate Highway Act of 1956, the system has cost roughly $350 billion to build, of which 90 percent has come from the federal government. Whether that amount is large or small depends very much on the calculation. Adjusted for inflation, the total cost to date is roughly a third higher than originally estimated. But most of the increase came from inflation in highway construction costs and expansions in the original design to accommodate population growth primarily in the South and West.

Moreover, one can easily argue that the benefits of the system far outweigh its costs. Lower accident rates saved billions of dollars in health costs and property losses, while the savings in time and

CHICAGO TRIBUNE

CHICAGO HISTORICAL SOCIETY

Laying concrete, 1954. Chicago's Eisenhower Expressway goes up as part of the federal government's vast expansion of the national highway system.

shipping costs and the thousands of new transportation jobs have helped the economy grow. Reduced accident rates also saved thousands of lives.

The interstate highway system continues to create its share of controversy. Some experts argue, for example, that the construction of more highways to combat congestion actually does just the opposite. In Washington, D.C., for example, between a quarter and half of all new roads are occupied by what experts call "induced travel" from commuters who take longer trips or switch from mass transit (buses, subways) to their own cars. Others believe that the time wasted in traffic jams and long job commutes should be counted as a cost of the interstate highway system, just as the time saved in shipping is counted as a benefit. Still others suggest that the money allocated to interstate highways could have been spent more wisely for developing light rail systems that would carry more riders at lower cost and less pollution and contribute less to the development of urban sprawl.

The federal government has done more than build the interstate highway system, however. It has also invested billions in helping states and localities build roads, bridges, and highways, much of which reflects the time-honored practice of pork barrel politics. The $217 billion Building Efficient Surface Transportation and Equity Act of 1998 (BESTEA) is only the latest in a long list of highway construction bills that provided federal aid back home.

The primary sponsor of the bill, twelve-term representative E. G. "Bud" Shuster (R-Penn.), refused to apologize for either the size of the measure, which increased federal transportation spending by nearly half, or its record-setting number of earmarks for special projects. Having warned his colleagues not to believe "this baloney that we somehow break the budget, that we somehow create a deficit," Shuster defended the $9 billion reserved for special projects earmarked by individual members of Congress. "Who knows better what is most important in their district than the Members of Congress from that district?" he asked of state officials who questioned the need for the earmarks. "I would respectfully suggest there is a bit of arrogance in those who say that somehow they know better what is important in their congressional districts than Members know. Indeed, I would suggest that if Members do not know what is really important to people in their congressional district, they are not going to be here very long."

Shuster reserved even harsher words for House colleagues who simultaneously attacked the projects even as they pushed for "multi-million dollar projects in their own congressional districts." "How I envy the pious," Shuster argued. "They can be such hypocrites and never even know it."

Last-minute negotiations leading to final passage of the bill proved his point. The Senate, which had long protested the earmarks as wasteful spending, offered a list of 360 projects worth $2.3 billion just hours before Congress was to adjourn for a long recess. "The Senate castigates projects," Shuster said. "But when they come to conference at about 2 a.m. on the twenty-first day, they reach in their pocket and pull out a list." Colleagues from both parties agreed. "Mr. Speaker, this is not pork," said a senior Democrat. "This is steak. If we want to continue to be a prime rib country, we better pass this bill quick."

Whether pork or steak, the nation could not hold together without the interstate highway system and the lesser connectors built with federal dollars. It is important to note, however, that the success of this endeavor may help explain the failure of the federal government's effort to strengthen urban mass transit. By building highways instead of mass transit systems such as subways and light rail, the federal government encouraged Americans to travel to and from work by car, thereby stimulating much of the urban sprawl that vexes commuters today, while diluting public support for urban mass transit. Thus does one endeavor's success sometimes precipitate another's failure.

8 Increase Health Care Access for Older Americans

Lyndon Johnson often receives credit for winning passage of the 1965 Medicare Act, which created an entirely new federal insurance program to provide health care access for older Americans. However,

To good health. Former president Harry S Truman shows the pens that President Lyndon Johnson used to sign the 1965 Medicare Act. The bill started with Truman and took almost twenty years to wind its way through the legislative process.

it was his predecessor, John F. Kennedy, who made Medicare for the elderly his top priority in 1961. Furthermore, the endeavor actually dates back to the late 1940s when Truman offered a much more comprehensive national health insurance program. Even Republican president Dwight D. Eisenhower helped move the issue along, if not by supporting legislative action, then at least by acknowledging that "I do not believe there is any use in shutting our eyes to the fact that the American people are going to get medical care in some form or other."

From the beginning of the debate, the major barrier to action centered on the 150,000 members of the American Medical Association (AMA), who were adamantly opposed to what they labeled as "socialized medicine," be it for all Americans or just the elderly. The

AMA claimed credit for defeating Truman's proposal in 1950 and kept health insurance off both party platforms in the 1952 and 1956 presidential elections.

The tide began to change in 1956 when labor unions won passage of a new Social Security program covering the totally and permanently disabled. With that victory in hand, the newly merged American Federation of Labor–Congress of Industrial Organizations (AFL-CIO) turned to national health insurance for the aged as the first step toward insurance for all citizens. Much as they tried to deflect the pressure by enacting a limited program of cash aid for the poor in 1960, Republicans could not stop the legislative momentum. Kennedy convened a White House conference on aging almost immediately after his inauguration and put Medicare at the top of his "New Frontier" agenda. By July 1961 the AFL-CIO had created the first national lobbying organization for the elderly, the National Council of Senior Citizens, and was busy producing 17 million pieces of literature arguing for action.

The AMA responded in kind, sending their members a poster for their offices entitled "Socialized Medicine and You," but was increasingly isolated in its opposition. The American Nurses Association endorsed Kennedy's plan in 1961, followed by the American Hospital Association early in 1962. Despite growing public support, Democrats did not have the votes on the key House Ways and Means Committee needed for passage, and Medicare soon slipped from the legislative agenda.

All that changed with the 1964 election, which brought sixty-five new Democrats to Congress. Emboldened by his landslide election, Johnson made Medicare his top priority, and congressional Democrats put the bill at the top of the legislative agenda in both chambers by numbering it H.R. 1 and S. 1. The final legislative debate over Medicare was almost anticlimactic. "It is obvious that the House is not in a mood to debate and deliberate," said one opponent on the House floor. "Members have already made up their minds. They are voting on a label." Knowing that the bill was destined to become law, almost half of the Republicans voted for its passage.

Johnson understood Medicare's lineage. He signed the bill at the Truman Library in Independence, Missouri, on July 30, 1965, and enrolled former President Truman and his wife, Bess, as the nation's first two Medicare recipients the same day.

Almost forty years later, Medicare covers nearly 40 million older Americans for the reasonable costs of all inpatient hospitalization, including drugs, surgery, and postoperative care. Like the Social Security program, these costs are covered by payroll taxes on individual citizens, which are set aside solely for Medicare expenditures in the Health Insurance Trust Fund. Also like the Social Security program, Medicare is financed on a pay-as-you-go basis. Current workers pay the taxes that cover the costs of current beneficiaries in return for promised benefits when they retire.

Unlike Social Security, however, Medicare beneficiaries can add to their coverage by purchasing additional federal health insurance to cover the costs of outpatient care, physician visits, and laboratory fees but not of prescription drugs. As of 2000 eligible beneficiaries paid about $46 a month for the supplementary insurance. Medicare beneficiaries must also pay a deductible on all hospital stays.

The good news about Medicare is that it has become a critically important source of health care for some of the nation's neediest citizens while giving beneficiaries a sense of security that they otherwise would not have. That security comes at a cost of $230 billion a year.

Unfortunately, that cost is rising much faster than revenues. Under current projections costs will exceed revenues sometime in the next fifteen years and continue rising through the 2020s. By 2030 almost a quarter of all Americans will be eligible for Medicare, driving the cost up from an amount equal to 2.6 percent of gross domestic product today to roughly 5.3 percent in 2040 and consuming roughly a third of the entire federal budget.

The financial crisis has three simple causes. First, the ratio of taxpayers to beneficiaries is about to fall rapidly as the huge baby boom starts to retire. By 2030 almost a quarter of all Americans will be eligible for Medicare. Second, life expectancy continues to rise, meaning that older Americans will draw benefits longer. This good news for older Americans is bad news of a kind for the Medicare budget. Third, medical costs are rising much faster than the rest of the economy, making Medicare the fastest growing item in the federal budget. Medicare costs would be rising even faster if Congress expanded the program to cover the costs of prescription drugs.

Because there are limits both to what current workers will pay even for a popular program such as Medicare and to what the elderly can afford in supplemental insurance payments, the federal government faces a series of tough choices to balance the program. That may mean using other sources of revenue to cover future costs or finding ways to cut health care costs. Nevertheless, Medicare will almost certainly still exist in 2050. Both parties recognize just how important the program has become to giving the elderly a healthy and secure retirement.

Even facing these cost pressures, Congress is almost certain to expand the Medicare program to cover prescription drugs, which can be prohibitively expensive for the elderly. By 2000 the question was no longer whether Medicare coverage would be expanded to include prescription drugs, but how much beneficiaries would have to pay in premiums for the coverage and how high the benefits would go.

9 Reduce the Federal Budget Deficit

Americans received some stunning news in the summer of 1999: the federal government had its first budget surplus in over twenty years. Although Congress and the president had set the process in motion with budget agreements in 1990, 1993, and 1997, the surplus showed up nearly three years ahead of schedule and much larger than expected. Even accounting for a brief recession sometime early in the 2000s, economic forecasters at both ends of Pennsylvania Avenue predicted that the surpluses would keep coming for at least the next ten years, adding up to more than $3 trillion total.

Although the long economic expansion of the 1990s had done much of the work by increasing employment, Congress and the president deserved much of the credit for restraining federal spending.

Stalemate! Disagreements over how to balance the budget in 1995 forced the shutdown of dozens of national parks and monuments, including this park near Las Vegas.

Between 1990 and 1998, the discretionary, or controllable, portion of the federal budget actually fell by 11 percent in real, inflation-adjusted terms. Although they did spend plenty of money on emergencies such as hurricanes, Congress and the president showed remarkable restraint over the decade. By doing nothing to spend new money, the government had produced a sizable part of the surplus.

Nevertheless, the surplus also reflected a good deal of just plain good luck. Almost everything went right for the budget during the 1990s. Companies saved billions on health care costs by shifting workers into health maintenance organizations and bargaining for lower fees from insurers, which resulted in higher wages for employees (which were taxed), higher earnings for shareholders (which were taxed), and higher corporate profits (which were taxed). The result was a dramatic increase in government revenue.

At the same time, the end of the cold war produced a 26 percent cut in defense spending over the decade and a highly successful effort to close obsolete military bases, which allowed Congress and the president to increase discretionary domestic spending by 24 percent without raising the deficit. Even income inequality seemed to help the budget: the fact that the rich got richer during the early 1990s meant that the federal government's progressive income tax brought in more revenue than otherwise expected.

The thirty-year effort to balance the budget was driven in large measure by the spending and investment required under many of the federal government's other endeavors. Building roads costs money, as does reducing disease, fighting wars, containing communism, strengthening the national defense, rebuilding Europe, ensuring safe food and drugs, and reducing poverty.

The effort was also driven by the huge tax cuts of 1981. Having won the presidential election by asking voters if they were better off in 1980 than they were four years earlier, President Reagan soon provided his own economic theory called supply-side economics. Contrary to the prevailing economic theories of the time, supply-side economics argued that federal tax cuts would actually reduce inflation while balancing the budget through an infusion of revenues stimulated by economic growth.

According to its advocates, the supply-side approach could only have its desired effects if the tax cuts went to the wealthy, who would then invest their newfound riches in the economy. In turn, those investments would build new factories that would employ millions of unemployed workers while flooding the consumer market with more goods, thereby simultaneously reducing unemployment *and* prices and marking an end to stagflation. Moreover, even as supply-side theory promised a lowering of the misery index (a combination of inflation and unemployment), it would also produce a balanced budget. Putting the unemployed to work meant a reduction in unemployment benefits, as well as an increase in tax revenues. Hence, lower taxes would actually produce higher revenues.

In fact, the 1981 tax cuts did exactly the opposite: They reduced federal government revenues dramatically. Coupled with the defense spending increases needed to fight the cold war, supply-side theory economics produced the largest federal budget deficits in American history. In turn, the deficits increased the federal debt, which drove interest rates upward, which eventually forced Congress and the president to undo the supply-side tax cuts and begin the hard work of balancing the budget.

Ultimately, reducing the budget deficit is almost entirely a function of political will, not legislative process. There is no process known to humankind that can stop Congress from spending money and cutting taxes if it so desires. In 1985, for example, Congress attempted to restrain itself by enacting the Balanced Budget and Emergency Deficit Control Act, which set annual targets for reducing the budget deficit. More commonly known as the Gramm-Rudman-Hollings Act in honor of its three sponsors—Phil Gramm (R-Tx.), Warren Rudman (R-N.H.), and Fritz Hollings (D-S.C.)—the law required the president to reduce the federal budget by a uniform percentage if Congress dared exceed the annual targets.

This "stop-me-before-I-kill-again" approach worked well until the budget ceilings were revised in 1990, just before they would have been exceeded. Facing an $85 billion across-the-board cut, Congress ignored the Gramm-Rudman-Hollings law and entered into negotiations with President George H. W. Bush on a package of tax increases and budget caps that yielded the first real steps toward success. In doing so, both parties showed the will needed to restrain spending. President George H. W. Bush violated his "read my lips: no new taxes" presidential campaign pledge, and Democrats accepted cuts in sacred-cow programs such as Medicare, welfare, and job training. Two additional compromises in 1993 and 1997 produced the first balanced budget in almost forty years.

Alongside these changes in budget law affecting *what* Congress spends, the effort to reduce the deficit also involved landmark legislation to change *how* the budget is debated. Under the Budget and Impoundment Control Act of 1974, Congress made four major changes in how the budget process works by

—sharply limiting the president's authority to impound, or refuse to spend, legally appropriated funding,

—creating its own independent source of budget information in the form of the Congressional Budget Office,

—establishing a new budget process designed to help the many committees and subcommittees involved in raising and spending money keep track of the bottom line, and

—creating new House and Senate budget committees to enforce the process.

At one level the act reduced the Congress's dependency on the president for basic information on how the federal bureaucracy is spending money. At a more fundamental level, however, the act reversed the delegation of power that had allowed presidents to impound funds in the first place. Although the Constitution had given Congress, not the president, responsibility for making spending decisions, Congress had delegated that power to the president by allowing impoundment under certain circumstances. Such delegations, which are usually done to help the president meet a national emergency or implement a particular law, sometimes grow into substantial sources of presidential power.

Despite the hopeful projections, reducing the budget deficit is a never ending challenge. First, roughly $2 trillion of the $3 trillion surplus is already promised to the baby boom generation in Social Security benefits that must be paid far into the future. Once the first of the 76 million baby boomers retires at age sixty-five in 2011, the federal government will need every last dollar it can get to cover the retirement costs.

Second, Congress spent $1.3 trillion of the hoped-for surplus on President George W. Bush's ten-year tax cut plan, another $40 billion on the New York City recovery, and yet another $35 billion on homeland defense. The Social Security costs, tax cut, and new spending add up to $3.4 trillion, or $400 billion *more* than the federal government is projected to have over the next ten years. In short, all the hard work getting to a balanced budget may have already been wasted, suggesting that the historians and political scientists might not rate *achievement of* the endeavor as highly today as they did when the surplus first appeared.

10 Promote Financial Security in Retirement

This endeavor was built around passage of the landmark 1935 Social Security Act. Starting out with barely 200,000 beneficiaries when the first checks were delivered in 1937, the program now provides benefits to 46 million Americans at an annual cost of more than $350 billion. Financed by a payroll tax on wages, the FICA (or Federal Insurance Contribution Act) tax is now collected from 152 million workers, compared to 46 million workers in 1937.

Social Security is not only the federal government's single largest program, it is also its most popular. Young Americans may have little confidence that they will ever see a penny in benefits from their contributions, and older Americans may worry about benefit cuts, yet they are adamant, as are all Americans, that the program be continued and expanded. So is the AARP (formerly the American Association of Retired Persons), whose 36 million members make it the largest lobbying group in the nation and one of the most feared.

Contrary to its image as a simple insurance program, Social Security is actually both an insurance program, in which citizens contribute "premiums" in the form of payroll taxes in return for retirement "annuities" in the form of monthly checks, and a welfare program, in which the benefit formula is weighted to give low-income beneficiaries a much higher "rate of return" on their taxes, thereby providing a floor against poverty.

Furthermore, Social Security is not a savings program, in which payroll taxes are invested in individual retirement accounts held in some great savings vault in Baltimore, Maryland, where the Social Security Administration is headquartered. To the contrary, Social Security is a classic pay-as-you-go-system, in which today's taxes are mostly spent on today's benefits. Social Security's financing depends almost entirely on having enough workers and employers paying taxes into the program to cover the benefits going out.

No one could have guessed how large those benefits would become when the Social Security Act was passed in 1935. The program technically began in 1937 with lump-sum payments to new retirees and only switched to monthly benefits in 1940. The first lump-sum payment of 17 cents went to a Cleveland retiree who applied for benefits one day after the program began.

As the program gained public support, Congress and the president began expanding the available benefits. Although the retirement age was set at sixty-five from the very beginning, virtually everything else about the program grew steadily over time. Bigger was always better.

In 1939, for example, Congress changed the benefit formula to increase the size of the first checks. Then it changed the benefit formula again in 1950, increasing benefit checks by roughly 77 percent. In 1956 Congress gave women the option to retire at age sixty-two and in 1961 allowed men to retire early, also. Finally, after three straight years of large annual benefit increases starting in 1969, Congress indexed benefits to an annual cost-of-living adjustment (COLA). It established the Supplemental Security Income (SSI) program in 1972 to provide additional cash payments to the elderly poor, and passed the Employee Retirement Income Security Act two years later to protect private pension plans.

Together these programs have increased financial security for older Americans while cutting the poverty rate in this group from 35 percent to just 12 percent between 1970 and 2000. Without Social Security almost half of Americans over the age of sixty-five would be living in poverty.

This is not to suggest that the trajectory has always been upward, however, or that Social Security is guaranteed for the future. As unemployment rose during the 1970s and Social Security tax revenues fell as a result, the program entered its first funding crisis in 1978. With Democrats in control of the White House and both houses of Congress, the rescue was simple: a nearly 2 percent tax increase to be phased in over fifteen years. President Jimmy Carter confidently predicted that the program was now safe for the next seventy-five years.

Unfortunately, the economy refused to cooperate. It responded instead with a new malady called "stagflation," a combination of high inflation that fattened Social Security benefit checks and stagnation that further depressed revenue through high unemployment. By 1981 the Social Security program was back in crisis, only this time with a Republican president in office and a Republican majority in the Senate. This time a rescue would not be so easy.

The rescue actually began in the worst way possible when the Reagan administration proposed a deep cut in Social Security benefits. When the proposal was denounced on both sides of the aisle and rejected by a 96-0 vote in the Senate, the Reagan administration hurriedly appointed a National Commission on Social Security Reform, chaired by future Federal Reserve Board chairman Alan Greenspan, to move the crisis off the front pages. Two years later the commission produced a $168 billion package of benefit cuts and tax increases to close the short-term deficit.

The compromise was the product of good old-fashioned politics. Business groups opposed any acceleration of the 1977 payroll tax increases, AARP opposed any benefit cuts, and labor unions opposed any increases in the retirement age. Because no one solution produced enough money by itself to solve the crisis, the commission had the makings of a compromise: Congress and the president would have to hurt all sides equally.

It was one thing to create the outlines of a compromise, however, and quite another to find the political cover to reach an agreement. With time running out on the commission in late December 1982, the White House and commission members created a secret "gang of nine" to develop the final package. Once adopted by the full commission, Congress could point to it as the cause of any pain, shifting the focus to an entity that had no forwarding address. Moreover, by wrapping their package in the red-white-and-bipartisan-blue of the commission, rescuers improved the odds that their plan would hold together on Capitol Hill. It is always easier to defend a bipartisan compromise than a secret deal.

Unfortunately, fixing Social Security in time to help the baby boom generation will make the 1983 rescue look like mere child's play. Although the 1983 package did contain an increase in the retirement age to sixty-seven, the demographic problems facing the program are formidable and easily illustrated by the ratio of workers to retirees. In 1935, for example, there were forty-six taxpayers for every beneficiary; today there are just three for one; by 2030 there will be two for one. By the 2010s the program will start spending more in benefits each year than it is scheduled to collect in taxes; by the 2030s it will exhaust that $2 trillion in savings it has been collecting over the past few years. At that point Social Security will be back in crisis.

The question is not whether Social Security will survive. Notwithstanding young Americans' doubts about ever seeing a penny of their taxes, the program is almost certain to exist well into the future. Rather, the question is when and how to fix the program. Congress could easily solve the future crisis by raising the retirement age to seventy over the next decade, boosting tax rates by half a percentage point or so, and reducing the annual COLA by a fraction.

Such advance planning is not yet on the legislative agenda, however. Unlike the 1983 rescue, which was framed by public panic about an immediate crisis, there is no intense pressure forcing Congress to act today. To the contrary, the Social Security surplus continues to grow as the baby boom generation continues to pay in far more than current retirees take out. By the time the nation actually realizes that it has a new Social Security crisis, it may be too late to do anything but raise taxes on younger generations or cut other domestic programs. With 50–60 million members by then, AARP most certainly will not accept any cuts in Social Security.

11 Improve Water Quality
and
15 Improve Air Quality

The Environmental Protection Agency is at the center of the federal government's recent effort to improve water and air quality. Although early legislative breakthroughs such as the 1948 Water Pollution Control Act and the 1963 Clean Air Act occurred under Democratic administrations, many of the nation's most important environmental statutes were signed into law by a Republican

Cleaning up the water. Federal funding spurred a dramatic expansion in the construction of sewage treatment plants starting in the 1960s.

president, Richard Nixon. Whereas earlier laws had given the federal government authority to work with states on developing antipollution plans, the 1960s brought a surge in public demand for national water and air quality laws such as the 1970 Clean Air amendments and the 1972 Clean Water Act.

Nixon's greatest contribution to environmental protection was not in signing those laws, however. It was in creating the Environmental Protection Agency to enforce those laws. With environmental protection spread across a dozen departments and agencies, Nixon realized that the federal government might well end up merely moving pollution from the air to the water and back again. Nixon pieced EPA together by combining the National Air Pollution Control Administration from what was then the Department of Health, Education, and Welfare, the Water Quality Administration from the Department of the Interior, and a number of other units and programs scattered across the rest of government.

The EPA and the laws it administers have improved environmental quality. Between 1978 and 1997, for example, the levels of five of the six airborne pollutants covered by the Clean Air Act fell dramatically. Carbon dioxide dropped 60 percent; nitrogen dioxide, 24 percent; smog, 30 percent; sulfur dioxide, 55 percent; and lead, 97 percent. It is hard to find a single city in America where the air quality is not significantly better today than it was when the EPA started making national regulations.

Rivers are also cleaner because of the Clean Water Act of 1972, which gave the federal government sweeping authority to regulate water pollutants, including chemical and industrial wastes as well as human sewage. That law was passed over President Nixon's veto and marked an entirely new approach to reducing pollution. Unlike the Water Pollution Control Act of 1948, which defined water pollution as primarily a state and local problem, the 1972 act defined pollution as an interstate problem demanding national action. States were ordered to purify all municipal and industrial wastewater before discharging it into rivers, streams, and lakes, and a national goal was established to make all water be "fishable" and "swimmable" as soon as possible.

The 1972 act and its 1977 amendments that govern toxic pollutants appear to have worked. In 1972 only a third of the nation's rivers and lakes were safe enough to use for fishing or swimming, and only 85 million Americans were served by sewage treatment plants. Lake Erie was dying, and Cleveland's Cuyahoga River was so contaminated that it actually caught fire in 1969. Today two-thirds of the nation's waters are safe to use, including the Cuyahoga, and wastewater treatment facilities now cover more than 170 million Americans.

The latest innovation in environmental protection involves greater public access to information on pollution in their communities. Under the 1986 Emergency Planning and Community Right to Know Act, for example, citizens can find out who is dumping what into their air, water, or landfills. The EPA's Toxic Release Inventory allows citizens to search for information by zip code, while its AIRNow website provides air pollution data for their communities, as well as basic information on the environmental effects of air pollution. The hope is that such locally accessible information will prompt businesses to clean up the air, water, and land *before* they reach the right-to-know list, rather than after. The more people know about threats to their own environment, the more they will demand action—at least according to the theory behind these laws.

Environmental protection comes at a cost, however, whether for new technologies to clean the air and water or for filing lawsuits against polluters. That is one reason why the federal government has started to experiment with different ways of encouraging businesses and other regulated parties to do the right thing naturally. Under the Clean Air Amendments of 1990, for example, Congress ordered the EPA to issue new rules that allowed coal-fired power plants to reduce their sulfur dioxide emissions in whatever way they deemed best. Rather than writing detailed regulations telling each plant how to scrub its smokestacks to remove the emissions that cause acid rain, EPA set a uniform target for every plant while allowing plants to buy and sell reductions with each other. By making cleanliness a product that can be bought and sold for profit, the new regulations produced significant gains in efficiency across the power industry as

BOHDAN HRYNEWYCH/STOCK BOSTON

WIDE WORLD

Dirty and clean. Federal air pollution laws have improved air quality across the nation. Although Los Angeles still has smoggy days like the one pictured here from the 1960s, it has more and more clear days, including this one from the late 1990s showing the spectacular mountains that surround the city.

a whole while reducing electricity costs by as much as $3 to $4 billion a year.

However, the EPA would be powerless without laws to enforce, and of these the Clean Air Act may be the most successful environmental statute ever enacted. Initially passed as the Air Pollution Control Act of 1955, which provided research grants to the states, the act has been expanded regularly over the years. The Clean Air Act of 1963 required the federal government to create health-based standards for reducing air pollution, while the 1970 amendments provided the basic structure of national standards to improve air quality. Under the 1970 amendments, considered the breakthrough laws for cleaning the air, the newly created Environmental Protection Agency set specific goals for reducing pollution, including the first limits on how much cars could pollute.

The Clean Air Act has produced measurable improvements in the environment. According to the EPA's Office of Air and Radiation, which administers the Clean Air Act, the results can be found in everything from clearer skies to cleaner rain. Virtually every emission regulated under the act has decreased. Emissions of toxic lead, which causes blood and respiratory illness, have been cut almost to zero, while every other measure of air quality has improved.

Over the past two decades, for example, the amount of acid rain has declined dramatically, largely due to the use of cleaner coal in midwestern power plants. The impact involves more than healthier lakes and streams in the Northeast, where most of the acid rain falls. It also prolongs the life of roads and bridges, homes and automobiles, all of which are spared the corrosive effects of the sulfuric acid that constitutes such a large proportion of the acid rain. Even as Congress and the president provided the funds to build the thousands of miles of federal and state highways, thereby increasing the number of automobiles on the road, the EPA was making sure that the air got cleaner by requiring reductions in exhaust gases emitted from those cars. These gases combine to form ground-level ozone and other pollutants. Unlike ozone in the upper atmosphere, which protects human beings from cancer-causing radiation, ozone at ground level is toxic and is a major component of that brown haze called smog.

The EPA still has plenty of work to do on clean air, however. Roughly 90 million Americans still live in what EPA classifies as "nonattainment areas," meaning parts of the country where poor air quality is considered a health risk. To attack that pollution, the 1990 amendments to the Clean Air Act gave the EPA sweeping new powers to set and enforce national air quality standards. Although states are free to set even tougher standards, which is exactly what California has done, they are not free to set lower standards. Indeed, if a state proves unwilling or unable to meet the federal minimums in a timely fashion, the 1990 act gives the EPA power to take over the state's responsibilities on behalf of its citizens.

12 Support Veterans' Readjustment and Training

The federal government has been involved in caring for its veterans of war since the very beginning of the Republic. With the Revolutionary War barely over, the Continental Congress established the nation's first programs to provide cash pensions to soldiers disabled in battle.

Once established, these programs expanded slowly but steadily as soldiers aged into disability and poverty. In 1818, for example, Congress expanded retirement benefits to cover all veterans of the Revolutionary War, whether officers or not, and created the first old soldiers' homes for poor veterans. By 1840 Congress expanded the veterans' program again to provide financial relief to the widows of soldiers killed in battle.

These early programs set two important precedents for contemporary domestic policy. First, they provided automatic benefits based on eligibility. As such, veterans' programs were the nation's first entitlement program, under which the government provides benefits to any citizen who is eligible. Second, these early programs restricted some benefits only to those citizens who could actually prove their need for help. As such, veterans' programs were the early examples of what are now called means-tested entitlements, under which citizens must prove they are poor enough to deserve the government's help.

Admitted. The federal government's GI bill gave veterans of World War II access to college. Here, veterans show their admission papers in September 1947.

Veterans' benefits are also important because they eventually came to cover huge numbers of Americans. The Civil War created much of the expansion. It was America's most extensive war, eventually involving some 2.2 million Union soldiers, many of whom became eligible for veterans' benefits after the war. (Congress never provided benefits to Confederate soldiers.)

Because so many men served in the Civil War and because benefits were even more generous for veterans of the Spanish-American War and World War I, America actually had no need for a social security system until the 1930s. It already had a huge national program that helped older Americans in need, provided they met the key entitlement criterion of veteran status. By 1932 veterans' benefits accounted for one quarter of all federal spending. Although that percentage has fallen steadily over the years as the World War II generation has passed on and new federal programs such as Social Security have expanded, the Department of Veterans Affairs will spend more than $40 billion in 2001 on a package of benefits that covers everything from health care to pensions and burial.

The most significant expansion of veterans' benefits occurred just before the end of World War II when Congress passed the Servicemen's Readjustment Act of 1944, better know as the GI Bill of Rights. The bill reflected intense lobbying by the American Legion and the growing awareness that the United States would soon confront the return of millions of veterans who would be looking for jobs in what was still a tight labor market.

The GI Bill sparked a vast expansion in home buying, job training, and education. In 1947 alone, veterans accounted for nearly half of all college enrollment. Out of 15 million eligible veterans, 8 million went to college or training programs at a cost of $15 billion. As the Department of Veterans Affairs itself acknowledges, "millions who would have flooded the labor market instead opted for education," which reduced unemployment as the U.S. economy adjusted to peace and prevented the civil unrest that would have occurred as civilians and veterans battled for the same jobs. According to a 1986 study by the Congressional Research Service, every dollar invested in the GI Bill produced between $5 and $12.50 in tax revenues from veterans whose college education gave them better jobs and higher salaries than they otherwise would have had.

It is important to note that this GI Bill was restricted to World War II veterans. Although the Veterans Administration and its network of hospitals, clinics, national cemeteries, and benefit offices have remained in place throughout the period, each new war brought a slightly larger GI Bill. The Vietnam Bill of Rights, for example, was signed into law on March 3, 1966, and required 180 days of continuous service after August 5, 1964. Alongside the already available health, education, and loan benefits, the Vietnam Bill of Rights provided funding to help veterans complete their high school education before going on to college, further augmenting the federal government's effort to improve access to postsecondary education.

Helping veterans readjust today is a more complicated task, in part because of the changing nature of war. Whereas it was relatively easy to determine whether a veteran qualified for a service-connected disability pension in World War II, when most injuries involved bullets and shrapnel, it has become much more difficult to make such determinations in an era of chemical warfare, mysterious illnesses such as Gulf war syndrome, and psychological illnesses such as post-traumatic stress disorder. Moreover, Vietnam veterans were so distrustful of the federal bureaucracy that the Veterans Administration had to invent an entirely new delivery system in the form of store-front service centers completely separate from the traditional VA health and benefit centers.

The question for the future is what to do with veterans' programs as the huge World War II generation passes on. By 2010 the number of veterans will be down sharply, as will demand for the health care provided by the federal government's 172 VA hospitals and hundreds of clinics. Some argue that the declining veteran population calls for a complete revision of how the nation delivers health care to former soldiers, perhaps even to the point of closing the hospitals in favor of a new Medicare option that would serve veterans alone.

The problem in such reforms, however, is that no one knows for sure what the future might bring in terms of military conflict. World

War I was supposed to be the war to end all wars, after all. Had the veterans system been dismantled after the armistice of 1919, Congress would have rebuilt it after December 7, 1941.

13 Promote Scientific and Technological Research

The federal government has been involved in *protecting* scientific and technological research from the moment the Constitution was ratified. Under Article I, Section 8, Congress was given the power to protect intellectual property by awarding patents and trademarks. It was a power that Congress used almost immediately in passing the Copyright Act of 1790, which prohibited states from awarding patents and copyrights, thereby declaring that the protection of intellectual property would be a federal responsibility.

It was not until the end of World War II, however, that the federal government became aggressively involved in *promoting* scientific and technological research. Convinced that research would help the United States win the cold war and attack a host of domestic problems such as reducing disease, Congress enacted the National Science Foundation Act in 1950, establishing a quasi-independent government agency (the NSF) fully dedicated to the support of basic research in all scientific and engineering disciplines. Starting out with the funding to award just 28 grants in 1952, NSF made more than 10,000 grants in 2000 and supports 20 percent of the research conducted at the nation's academic institutions. Although NSF grants can be sizable, the agency tends to spread its $4.5 billion across a very large number of relatively small projects, almost all of which are conducted by university-based researchers.

In the fairly typical week of October 22, 2001, for example, NSF made thirty-four grants totaling more than $2 million, covering everything from the role of aquifers in paleoclimatic reconstructions of glaciated watersheds to the physics of transition metal oxides and related materials. The NSF also launched five "quick-response" projects to examine the human and social impacts of the September 11 terrorist attacks, including a study on whether and how memories of what happened on September 11 will change over

Building a network. The inventors of the Internet use tin cans, zucchini, and string to compare their primitive ARPANET to today's high-speed information highway.

time. One of the NSF studies actually produced its first results within weeks of the tragedies, showing that Americans responded with a surge of national pride, faith in people, and a readiness to help others.

Congress continued to expand the research infrastructure in 1958 when it provided funding for creation of the Advanced Research Projects Agency (ARPA), which was designed to maintain a lead in applying state-of-the-art technology to military problems and prevent technological surprise from U.S. adversaries. Now known as the Defense Advanced Research Projects Agency, or DARPA, the agency has completed thousands of projects over the decades, many of which contributed to the end of the cold war.

With a budget of $2 billion a year, DARPA is roughly half as large as the NSF but tends to concentrate its funding on very large projects that are often conducted by private contractors whose work is classified as top secret. Although that work often produces breakthroughs of great public value, DARPA rarely gets the credit, which is exactly how the agency wants it. Whereas the NSF lists every grant it makes on its website, DARPA only provides news releases when it wants the public to know something important has happened.

DARPA's most famous project involved development of a computer network that eventually became the Internet. Although Vice President Al Gore once jokingly claimed credit for having invented the Internet, he was only a teenager when DARPA began examining a new form of information sharing called "packet switching," in which computers could send packets of information back and forth across a network. Because long-distance telephone connections were prohibitively expensive, DARPA eventually decided to invest in a cable network to link the growing number of high-speed computer centers across the country. That network, called ARPANET, was launched in 1967.

The ARPANET was never exclusively a federal effort, however. Rather, it involved a vibrant partnership between the federal government, university scientists, and private firms. ARPANET was actually built by a Cambridge, Massachusetts, computer design firm called Bolt, Bernake, and Newman, and it was originally designed only to link computers at Stanford, the University of California at Los Angeles, the University of California at Santa Barbara, and the University of Utah. As the concept developed, other universities were added to the network.

By 1973 the team had solved what they called the "internetting problem," which appears to have been the first time the word *internet* was used. Ten years later 400 computers had been connected through a series of separate regional networks. Three years later still, in 1986, the National Science Foundation created NSFNet, which provided the high-speed backbone for today's Internet. Even then the Internet could not be a reality until someone figured out how users could switch from site to site.

This "browsing" problem fell to an undergraduate student working at the National Center for Supercomputing Applications at the University of Illinois. Working with funding from the National Science Foundation, Marc Andreesen designed a point-and-click browser named NCSA Mosaic. Andreesen eventually left college to create a firm called Netscape in 1994.

The NSF and DARPA are not the only places where research is conducted or promoted, however. The federal government launches thousands of new projects every year, including deep space research at NASA, highway safety research at the Department of Transportation, environmental risk analysis at the EPA, and medical research at the NIH.

In 1991, for example, Congress provided the funding to support the Human Genome Project, a fifteen-year project designed to decode the basic building blocks of life, DNA, at a cost of $3 billion. A working draft of the entire human genome sequence was completed in June 2000, and numerous private firms are working off earlier advances in gene splicing to create drugs and therapies that may help the United States conquer illnesses such as Parkinson's and Alzheimer's disease and cancer.

14 Contain Communism

The United States spent the better part of the twentieth century fighting a long, cold war with the Soviet Union and communism. Although the conflict involved plenty of killing, including more than 100,000 U.S. casualties in the Korean and Vietnam Wars, it was

WIDE WORLD

An elusive enemy. U.S. soldiers slog through the jungle looking for their enemy somewhere in South Vietnam. More than 50,000 troops gave their lives fighting what turned out to be an unwinnable war against communism in that country.

called the cold war because it never involved a battle between U.S. and Soviet forces.

Although China and Cuba are still controlled by communist governments today, the United States succeeded in stopping the spread of communism to Western Europe and Africa and won the cold war with the Soviet Union. With its economy in ruins, its citizens frustrated by endless food shortages and inflation, and its allies breaking away to pursue their own independent course, the Soviet Union finally gave up its failed experiment with totalitarianism in 1989.

Along the way the United States fought two major wars, one to defend South Korea from a Soviet-sponsored invasion by North Korea and another to defend South Vietnam from a Soviet-supported war that began with guerillas in the south and escalated to a full engagement with the North Vietnamese. Both wars resulted in heavy U.S. casualties and stalemate. The Soviet Union also fought its wars, most notably a long and brutal engagement in Afghanistan that became known as its Vietnam. Both nations spent billions to maintain large armies stationed around the world, while building huge arsenals of nuclear weapons that could destroy the world many times over.

The fall of communism had begun in the mid-1980s, five years before the Berlin Wall separating East and West Berlin fell under a thousand sledgehammers in 1989. By the mid-1980s the Soviet economy was already straining under the effort to keep up with U.S. military might. By the time Mikhail Gorbachev rose to power as the Soviet Union's last leader, his country was on the verge of complete economic collapse.

In a last-minute effort to save the union, Gorbachev imported two democratic ideas. The first was a policy of *glasnost*, or freedom of speech; the second was *perestroika*, or economic rebuilding. Gorbachev soon recognized that Russia could never hold the Soviet Union together against the growing internal dissent and burgeoning demand for freedom.

By 1987 the Baltic states of Estonia, Lithuania, and Latvia had broken free of their former master to the east and were soon followed by Poland, Hungary, and the rest of the Eastern European nations the Soviets had captured at the end of World War II. On December 25, 1991, Gorbachev gave his people the ultimate Christmas present by resigning, thereby declaring the Soviet Union dead. Although the military tried ever so briefly to regain control, the union was over. "Once the forces of glasnost and democracy were let loose," Gorbachev wrote in 1999, "they worked in unpredictable ways." On the one hand, they guaranteed the end of communism and the triumph of freedom. On the other, with no military government to suppress dissent and disagreement, the new liberty unleashed intense ethnic conflict in nations such as in Yugoslavia and other Balkan states. The slaughter of innocent women and children by Serbian forces in Kosovo eventually drew the United States into an air war in 1999.

The United States won the cold war for three reasons. First, it was willing to "pay any price, bear any burden," as Kennedy had put it, to defend freedom anywhere in the world. It was ready to spend any amount of money to make sure the United States had the military might to fight communism on all fronts. The Soviet Union simply did not have the economic resources to make the same promise to defend communism anywhere in the world. Second, the United States had the moral high ground in the battle. As Gorbachev found out, freedom is a nearly irresistible product. Once human beings experience it, they simply cannot accept the kind of control implied in communism.

The United States also won the cold war because it had the consent of its governed, whereas the Soviet Union did not. Although there were moments when the public withdrew some of that consent, particularly during the Vietnam War, the American people were the ones who were ultimately willing to pay any price and bear any burden.

There were stinging defeats along the path to victory. Convinced that the fall of South Vietnam would lead to the fall of Southeast Asia, toppling a long chain of dominoes that would eventually lead to the fall of its own government, the United States entered what would become its longest and most unpopular war. Starting with a handful of military advisers in 1959 and rising to a force of more than 500,000 troops in 1965, the United States went to war against an enemy that had been fighting for independence for the better part of two centuries.

In retrospect, the effort was doomed from the beginning. Despite President Kennedy's inaugural promise that the United States would pay any price and bear any burden to defend freedom, the American public was not ready to support a long and costly war in a distant land, especially one waged by such a tenacious, often hidden adversary. As the casualties mounted, America's college and university campuses became the center of an increasingly violent antiwar movement, which added to the civil unrest already under way in the nation's cities.

The South Vietnamese people also seemed to have doubts about fighting the war. Many of the guerillas who fought in the war against the United States had grown up in South Vietnam and joined the resistance to fight their country's own corrupt government. Having assumed that it could build a democracy in South Vietnam where one had never existed before, the United States never quite succeeded, installing one flawed leader after another. The early failure to "Vietnamize" the war by turning over the fighting to the South Vietnamese army further undermined the American public's confidence back home. It was one thing to help a brave nation defend itself from communism; quite another to assist a corrupt government that had no intention of fighting a war for freedom.

On top of these political problems, the United States flatly misread the costs of a guerilla war with a deeply entrenched adversary. The military had assumed that the North Vietnamese army would stand up and fight a conventional war, meaning one in which each side would take defined positions that could be defended and attacked. Instead, the Vietnam War was fought on a shifting battleground as the Viet Cong moved from skirmish to skirmish, engaging the United States for a moment or two, then disappearing back into a maze of tunnels and hiding places. Frustrated by this evasive enemy, U.S. troops began to see a potential Viet Cong threat in every South Vietnamese face.

The turning point in the war came on January 31, 1968, when the Viet Cong joined with North Vietnamese troops to launch a coordinated offensive at the start of Tet, the Vietnamese celebration of the lunar new year. Televised pictures of U.S. troops fighting desperately to recapture the American embassy building in downtown Saigon convinced many Americans that the Vietnam War could not be won, reinforcing what some observers labeled the "credibility gap" between the promise and reality of U.S. engagement. When his military commanders asked for another 206,000 troops, Johnson said no. Only weeks later he withdrew from the 1968 presidential campaign, convinced that it was an election he could not win.

The war ended seven years later in 1975 when North Vietnamese troops finally destroyed the last remnants of the South Vietnamese army, and President Gerald Ford declared the war "finished." All totaled, it involved 2.2 million American soldiers, of whom more than 58,000 died, and cost billions that might have been invested in winning the war on poverty that began in the mid-1960s. The war also produced what some foreign policy experts call the "Vietnam syndrome," which is the tendency of U.S. military commanders to avoid all engagements that might produce another long, unwinnable war, and a backlash from Congress against what it saw as an abuse of the war power by Johnson.

Much as one should celebrate the nation's success in containing communism, the end of the cold war has brought a new uncertainty to American foreign policy. President Clinton captured the sentiment perfectly in 1993 when he said, "Gosh, I miss the cold war." Many U.S. policymakers shared his view. It was not that they longed for the nuclear tensions of the 1960s or that they wanted to wage new wars in distant lands. Rather, they recognized that the world had become a far more complicated place for making foreign policy. Whereas the United States used to set its national interest in opposition to the Soviet Union, it must now think hard about where and how to engage. It must be clearer about the problems it wants to solve, the tools it has to deploy, and the ongoing implementation of its foreign policies.

16 Enhance Workplace Safety

As with so many of its greatest endeavors of the past fifty years, the federal government's involvement in protecting workers from unsafe conditions dates back to the late 1700s. Congress passed the first worker protection act in 1790 to protect merchant seamen from danger at sea. Although the act allowed the majority of a ship's crew to force an unseaworthy vessel to the nearest port if they could get the first mate to agree, there is no evidence that any crew ever mustered the courage for such potentially mutinous action.

Congress became more aggressive in 1917 when it created the Department of Labor, in part to improve working conditions. The Senate specifically asked the first secretary of labor to report on industrial diseases and accidents, which he did through what is now called the Bureau of Labor Statistics. To this day, the bureau provides yearly reports on accidents and deaths across industries. It was not until the 1960s, however, that Congress imagined a significant federal role in actually regulating workplace safety. That responsibility had always belonged to the states. Although Congress did pass a 1935 law setting minimal safety standards for workers on federal projects and a 1958 amendment covering merchant seamen, who were obviously not covered by any one state, it steered clear of broader standards until a series of devastating mine accidents led to passage of the Federal Mine Safety Act of 1969.

Mines were not the only source of injury, however. In 1970 alone nearly 14,000 workers died from job-related injuries, including 425 deaths in mining accidents, while another 2.2 million were injured. Exposure to lead, cotton dust (which produces "brown lung" disease), coal dust ("black lung" disease), asbestos, and other toxic substances that year cost the U.S. economy $1.5 billion in lost wages, another $8 billion in lost productivity because of absenteeism, and unknown amounts in higher health spending and federal disability payments to victims.

After three years of wrangling between labor unions and business groups, Congress finally passed the Occupational Safety and Health

The Farmington, West Virginia, mine disaster. Flames from the 1968 disaster rose 75 feet (note the helicopter above the smoke). The accident propelled efforts to create the Occupational Safety and Health Administration.

Act in 1970. The act ordered the federal government to create national safety standards governing everything from wearing hard hats in construction zones to the use of automatic shutoff switches on industrial machinery. The act also created the Occupational Safety and Health Administration (OSHA) within the Department of Labor with responsibility for enforcing the standards through an inspection and citation program.

The Occupational Safety and Health Act was passed by close margins in both houses and signed into law by Richard Nixon, creating yet another example of how divided government can produce significant successes. Thirty years after its creation, OSHA can claim most of the credit for halving the overall workplace death rate. OSHA action is also credited with reducing the number of deaths caused by on-the-job accidents in a number of high-risk industries. From 1980 to 1995, for example, the number of work-related deaths fell from 7.5 per 100,000 workers to 4.3 per 100,000. According to OSHA, deaths from construction trench cave-ins have fallen by a third since the 1970s, blood poisoning among battery plant and smelter workers has fallen by two-thirds, and brown lung disease among textile workers has been virtually eliminated.

Despite these successes, OSHA is often the target of harsh criticism, largely from the businesses it regulates. It has tried to address some of the criticism by becoming a more active partner in helping businesses find ways to reduce workers' compensation costs and lost workdays. It now seeks voluntary compliance with its workplace standards by showing businesses how they can save both money and lives by implementing simple safety procedures—everything from setting ladders more securely to new standards for protecting taxi drivers from robberies.

OSHA's greatest challenge in the immediate future is reducing musculoskeletal disorders such as carpal tunnel syndrome, which comes from repetitive tasks such as computer data entry or grocery scanning. These disorders are the fastest growing, most expensive, yet most easily preventable workplace injury of the information era.

The challenge is to craft a rule that might reduce injuries without inflicting unnecessary costs on businesses, thereby balancing costs against benefits. Although OSHA argues that its proposed "ergonomics rule" to reduce injuries from heavy lifting, repetitive stress, and a host of other task-related injuries will generate $15 billion in benefits, some business interest groups estimate that the rule will cost $50–$100 billion to implement, tipping the cost-benefit ratio sharply to the negative. As of this writing, the debate over the cost-benefit ratio continues, suggesting that the issue is likely to be resolved in Congress, not the agency.

This kind of controversy is one sign of OSHA's significant impact on the workplace. Much as it tries to satisfy its many customers, OSHA's primary task is to implement laws designed to save lives and protect workers, even if doing so costs money.

Today OSHA's 1,200 regulators and 1,100 inspectors are involved in protecting virtually every employee in the nation, including the hundreds of construction workers who cleaned up the devastation of the World Trade Center attacks. Workers at "ground zero," as the site quickly became known, were required to wear protective clothing and breathing equipment to protect themselves against asbestos, silica, mercury, and other pollutants that were mixed into what remained of the 110-story buildings. Of the hundreds of samples of dust collected in the days following the attack, OSHA found asbestos in more than a quarter, which triggered existing regulations governing worker protection.

17 Strengthen the National Defense

One of the reasons the United States won the cold war is that it built the world's most expensive defense system and challenged the Soviet Union to keep up. The United States committed to both quantity and quality, investing in sophisticated new technologies such as stealth, or radar-evading, aircraft while purchasing more of virtually every item on the defense menu.

Air superiority was just one result. During the 1991 Gulf war, the U.S. Air Force lost exactly one fighter in air-to-air combat, and its premier fighter, the F-15C, flew 6,000 missions without a single

©BETTMANN/CORBIS

The new defense. Maintaining a strong defense has become a high-tech effort. The soldier pictured here is relaying the position of enemy tanks to air and ground support.

casualty, saving lives that might have been lost in less sophisticated aircraft and securing a quicker end to the war.

Maintaining the world's greatest defense system is expensive, however. The federal government currently spends more than four times as much on defense as Russia or China, and the defense budget remains roughly 80 percent as large as it was at the height of the cold war. That is how much it costs to maintain the forces needed to fight two land wars in different parts of the world at the same time while sustaining a research and development program to make sure U.S. weapons keep pace with the latest technology.

In 1999, for example, Congress was asked to commit $40 billion for further development and purchase of 339 F-22 Raptors, a high-speed, high-tech, stealth fighter plane. With the forward fuselage built by the Lockheed Martin Corporation in Marietta, Georgia; the mid-fuselage made by Lockheed Martin in Fort Worth, Texas; the wings built by Boeing in Seattle; the engines assembled by Pratt & Whitney at several plants around the country; and the computers and weapons systems provided by a variety of contractors, the decision had big impacts all across the country. Although Congress initially decided to spend the money on less sophisticated equipment, it finally agreed to purchase a smaller number of F-22s following a furious lobbying campaign by the Lockheed Corporation.

That fight was tame compared to the battle over the Joint Strike Fighter (F-35), which will replace the existing Air Force F-16s and A-10s, Navy F/A-18s, and the Marine Corps AV-8B Harriers, all of which were involved in the war over Kosovo and Afghanistan. It will be the fighter for all wars, able to launch from land and sea and to return to runways long and short. All totaled, the United States plans to buy more than 3,000 planes by 2040. At a cost of $200 billion in sales to the United States alone, the F-35 will be the most expensive piece of defense hardware ever purchased.

The contest over who will build the aircraft involved two giant defense contractors, Lockheed Martin and Boeing, both of which had been given large federal contracts in 1996 to design prototypes of the radar-evading, or stealth, airplane. With 9,000 jobs and thirty years of profit at stake, including foreign sales that will equal at least another $200 billion, both companies worked tirelessly to make the sale. In the end the Defense Department decided on Lockheed Martin. Although the department toyed with splitting the contract to give Boeing a piece of the action, the Pentagon's chief planners decided to put the whole project in the hands of just one contractor. However, within days of the decision, which came in the midst of the Afghanistan air war, members of Congress began fighting over it, in part under pressure from Boeing lobbyists to rescue something from the competition.

With much of the equipment purchased in the 1980s now wearing out, there is growing agreement that the United States must make tough choices to maintain its military readiness. It can either build highly sophisticated systems such as the F-22, or it can spend the money to ensure it gets enough young Americans to volunteer for the armed services; buy the spare parts to maintain the old fighters, tanks, and ships; and purchase the occasional new system needed to keep the United States so far ahead of its adversaries that they dare not pick a fight. Unless the public suddenly decides that it prefers guns to butter (domestic social programs), foreign-policymakers will have to choose.

It is one thing to have modern equipment but another to be able to coordinate its use by the Army, Navy, Air Force, and Marine Corps during battle. That is why part of maintaining a strong defense has involved building a stronger, more effective Department of Defense. Having established the Defense Department in 1947, Congress has returned repeatedly to defense organization over the decades, always striving to create what Eisenhower described as "real unity" across the services. Congress responded with the first of several Defense Department reorganizations in 1958, creating the Joint Chiefs of Staff to direct the actual armed forces. Although the Defense Department would still contain three separate subdepartments for Army, Air Force, and Navy (which contains the Marine Corps), the goal was a unified command that would control all actions of soldiers, sailors, and pilots during war.

Congress continued the effort to coordinate the four services with a landmark reorganization in 1986. Under the Department of Defense Reorganization Act, Congress gave the chairman of the Joint Chiefs of Staff even more power to direct the armed forces of the four services. The bill also shifted power upward from the separate military departments to the secretary and deputy secretary of the Defense Department, thereby reducing the interservice rivalries that had so often plagued battlefield cooperation. According to many observers, U.S. success in the Gulf war, Kosovo, and Afghanistan was the direct result of tighter coordination from the top.

Whatever Congress and the president decide regarding future defense spending and organization, the United States is not likely to lose its status of having the world's greatest defense system. Having won the cold war in part by blending new systems into the old, the United States will likely respond to its current challenge in the same way, giving it just enough of an edge to reduce the loss of life if it has to go to war.

18 Reduce Hunger and Improve Nutrition

For most of U.S. history, the nation relied on private charities and local governments to feed the hungry. That began to change during the Great Depression when these traditional providers were overwhelmed by soaring unemployment and poverty. Although the federal government did not create a permanent food program until after World War II, Congress did authorize the Federal Surplus Relief Corporation to start purchasing surplus agriculture products for needy families in 1935, which in turn led to the nation's first school lunch programs.

By 1941 more than 5 million children were receiving free school lunches, consuming more than 450 million pounds of surplus pork, dairy products, and bread. Although the program was disbanded during World War II because of food shortages, it was restored under the 1946 National School Lunch Act. As Truman said at the signing ceremony, "no nation is any healthier than its children." He also could have added that hunger had been a national security issue during the war because of the high rejection rate of draftees due to malnutrition.

The school lunch program set the stage for two major expansions in the federal effort to reduce hunger over the next thirty years. The first came with creation of the Food Stamp Program, which is a classic example of a proposal that passed because two very different interest groups united around a single policy goal. Ordinarily, the agricultural lobby and antipoverty groups would never work together. Agricultural groups mostly represent individual farmers and giant food processors such as Archer Daniels Midland who share almost nothing in common with the interest groups that support more federal spending for the poor. But they came together for a

STEVE LEHMAN/SABA

WIC at work. The 1972 Special Supplemental Food Program for Women, Infants and Children (WIC) uses food coupons to provide a balanced diet to pregnant women, mothers, and young children.

brief moment in 1964 to create what one scholar has labeled "the most important change in public welfare policy in the United States since the passage of the Social Security Act in 1935."

That change was the Food Stamp Act, which set up a program to provide eligible low-income families with coupons to be used to purchase food. In 1999 roughly 18 million Americans used food stamps at some time during the year to help them buy food. Roughly half of the Americans who benefit from the program are children. Although food stamps cannot be used to purchase alcohol, tobacco, soap, toothpaste, or toilet paper, some food stamps are used to purchase junk food. That is why the Department of Agriculture, which administers the program, also works to educate Americans about the components of a healthy diet.

The idea of giving food coupons to low-income families actually emerged during the Great Depression as a way to distribute surplus food, such as cheese, rice, and flour, that the federal government had bought to stabilize farm prices. The program was abandoned during World War II when food surpluses dropped sharply, but emerged again in the 1950s when agriculture groups convinced Congress to pass new farm price supports.

By the 1960s the federal government was buying and distributing so many agricultural products that it was becoming a major food consumer itself, storing millions of tons of food in federal warehouses around the country. The modern Food Stamp Program was proposed as a way to get the federal government out of the commodity business while giving poor Americans easier access to food. Instead of lining up at a federal warehouse to get a brick of surplus cheese or bag of surplus rice, the Food Stamp Program would allow poor Americans to purchase a wide variety of products off the same grocery shelves that other Americans use.

When the proposal came to the floor of the House, advocates for the poor offered a simple deal: they would support continuation of price supports for the agriculture lobby if the lobby would support creation of the Food Stamp Program. With strong support from southern Democrats and midwestern Republicans, both of whom represented agriculture, and northeastern Democrats, who represented many of the nation's poorest cities, the Food Stamp Program moved through Congress with little opposition.

The greatest challenge facing the program today is making sure that all eligible Americans receive their benefits. According to a 1999 study by the Urban Institute, a think tank in Washington, D.C., roughly two-thirds of the families that left the program in 1997–98 were actually still eligible for benefits. Having left welfare for work, these recipients mistakenly assumed that they were no longer eligible for the program when, in fact, families can remain on food stamps as long as total household income does not exceed $1,500 a month.

Despite these challenges, the Food Stamp Program continues to enjoy enormous support in Congress and the interest group community. Farmers and food processors recognize that it is easier to have poor Americans buy food at the grocery store than deal with a federal warehouse, while advocates for the poor recognize that there is a measure of dignity in giving hungry Americans the freedom to shop with the rest of the nation.

Ten years later Congress created a second major nutritional program called the Special Supplemental Nutrition Program for Women, Infants, and Children. Long known simply as WIC, the program celebrated its twenty-fifth anniversary in 1999 as one of the federal government's most successful antipoverty programs.

WIC was designed to address a very specific group of poor Americans. As explained by the Department of Agriculture's Food and Nutrition Service, which administers the program, the primary mission is "to safeguard the health of low-income women, infants, and children up to age 5 who are at nutritional risk by providing nutritious foods to supplement diets, information on healthy eating, and referrals to health care." WIC was built around hard scientific evidence that weight gain during a mother's pregnancy correlates strongly with the birth weight of the baby and thus its survival, and that weight gain in the first years of life is linked to a child's physical and emotional well-being. Hence WIC concentrates its efforts on improving nutrition for pregnant women and their young children.

In its twenty-fifth year, WIC served 7.5 million women and children through $4 billion in grants to state governments to provide access to supplemental foods. WIC also promotes breast-feeding by new mothers and funds nutrition education and referrals to health care and social service providers. WIC food packages consist of iron-fortified infant formulas, milk, cheese, eggs, iron-fortified adult and infant cereals, fruit and vegetable juices rich in vitamin C, dried peas or beans, and peanut butter, thereby adding important nutrients lacking in low-income diets: protein, vitamins A and C, calcium, and iron. By law 80 percent of WIC funds must be spent on food.

The available evidence shows that WIC works. Research published by the federal government shows that participation in the program increases birth weights among newborn infants, reduces iron-deficiency anemia in children, and may increase the likelihood that mothers take their children to health providers for immunization against childhood diseases such as measles. In addition, participation may also reduce the costs to government of early health problems among low-birth-weight babies, thereby helping pay for the program indirectly.

As part of its effort to promote good nutrition, WIC began providing special funding in 1992 for the purchase of fresh produce at farmers' markets across the country. Although each WIC recipient only receives a small amount per month under the program, the goal is to give needy mothers a reliable source of fruits and vegetables. By 2000 roughly 12,000 farmers and 1,500 farmers' markets were participating in the program.

19 Increase Access to Postsecondary Education

Under the GI Bill, the federal government may have made its greatest commitment to helping Americans go to college. The federal government not only paid for tuition, it also paid for books and education materials and contributed to living expenses. Before the GI Bill, however, Washington had left the financing of college education to the states, private citizens, and philanthropists. Although Congress did give states and territories huge amounts of federal land for the foundation and support of what became known as land-grant colleges, it had no interest in helping students pay the tuition to those colleges.

Despite these precedents, it was not until the late 1950s that Congress and the president came to believe that the federal government needed to create new opportunities for postsecondary education. Eisenhower launched the discussion in 1955 with a White House Conference on Education, which broached the subject of federal support for college construction and general loans but did not endorse any specific program.

The conversation became much more urgent after the Soviet Union launched Sputnik on October 9, 1957. Suddenly the federal government's role in supporting scientific and technical education became a national concern. On November 7, 1957, Eisenhower told the American public that the shortage of trained scientists and engineers was "one of our greatest and most glaring deficiencies" in winning the new space race. Less than a week later, he told the public that the Soviet Union had an edge in both fields and was currently "producing graduates . . . at a much faster rate." Two months later still, Eisenhower asked Congress to fund 10,000 college scholarships each year for four years, with preference given to students who showed an interest in science and engineering.

The panic over Sputnik eventually led Congress to enact the National Defense Education Act of 1958. Ironically, the final bill did not contain a single one of Eisenhower's proposed scholarships. What it did contain was $1 billion in long-term low-interest loans for needy students, matching funds for purchase of scientific teaching aids and laboratory equipment, and money for graduate fellowships. As the preamble to the act declared, "The Congress hereby finds and declares that the security of the Nation requires the fullest development of the mental resources and technical skills of its young men and women."

All that was left was to give a postsecondary form and substance to the commitment. That task fell to Kennedy and Johnson, both of whom labored to win passage of legislation opening college to all students, regardless of race, gender, or age. Both presidents also committed the nation to helping needy students fund their college education through federal direct scholarships and grants that did not have to be repaid. Under the Higher Education Act of 1965, Congress created the first federal scholarships for disadvantaged students. Called educational opportunity grants, the scholarship covered tuition expenses of up to $800 a year, which at that time was more than enough to cover the cost of college. Congress also gave states the money to insure loans to students made by commercial lenders, as well as additional funding under a 1963 law to aid in construction of classrooms, dormitories, libraries, and research facilities to accommodate the growing number of baby boomers entering college in the 1960s.

All totaled, the original act has been reauthorized six times, most recently in 1998. Under the 1998 amendments, the Pell Grant Program, named in honor of its creator, Senator Claiborne Pell (D-R.I.), was increased slightly to cover more tuition. In addition, Congress created the Academic Achievement Incentive Scholarships for students who graduate in the top 10 percent of their high school classes.

Congress also used the amendments to pursue other endeavors. It ordered colleges and universities to make "a good faith effort" to distribute a mail voter registration form to each student and required much more detailed reporting on campus crime. Institutions are currently required to report murder, manslaughter, rape, arson, armed robberies, and other violent property crimes, as well as hate crimes in which victims are targeted because of actual or perceived race, gender, religion, sexual orientation, ethnicity, or disability.

It is difficult to dispute the impacts of these efforts to increase access to higher education, especially for disadvantaged Americans. More than 60 percent of all lower-income students in college today have a federal grant of some kind, while more than 70 percent of all Pell grants go to students who earn less than $9,000 a year on their own or whose families earn $20,000 a year or less.

20 Enhance Consumer Protection

Few Americans have had a more dramatic impact in pressuring government to protect consumers than Ralph Nader. Starting with his best-selling 1967 book, *Unsafe at Any Speed*, Nader pushed for federal action on a host of public interest issues, from automobile safety to contaminated food, air pollution, deceptive advertising, and campaign finance reform. "Until Nader came on the scene," one of his allies explained, "the common pattern on the Hill with consumer legislation was for the sponsors to introduce the strongest bill they could conceive of passing and then hold on for dear life while it got whittled away during its passage through both houses." By educating the public on the need for action through his network of public

AP/WIDE WORLD/JEFF ZELEVANSKY

Pokémon in retreat. Working with the Consumer Product Safety Commission, Burger King recalled millions of Pokémon toys following the death of a 13-month-old who suffocated when the ball containing the toys covered her mouth and nose.

interest research groups, Nader improved the odds that consumer legislation would emerge intact.

The Consumer Product Safety Commission (CPSC) survives to this day as a testament to Nader's success as a public interest lobbyist. Created by law in 1972, the CPSC is required to "protect the public against unreasonable risks of injuries and death associated with consumer products." With jurisdiction over nearly 15,000 consumer items, from toasters to bike helmets, lawn mowers, and child car seats, the CPSC often relies on consumers, the media, and manufacturers to bring potential problems to its attention. Manufacturers are also required by law to tell the CPSC about product defects that might create a substantial risk of consumer injury. The CPSC also monitors injuries caused by consumer products via its National Electronic Injury Surveillance System, which collects data from hospital emergency rooms across the country.

Once it proves that a product is actually dangerous, the CPSC has the power to issue a recall order. A recall is a simple term covering the removal, repair, replacement, or refund of an unsafe product. In early 2000, for example, the CPSC spurred the recall of nearly 25 million toy Pokémon balls that Burger King had included in its kids' meals. The balls, which split in half to reveal a Pokémon toy, were blamed for the suffocation deaths of two infants and were considered an immediate hazard. Under its recall agreement with the CPSC, Burger King notified its customers of the hazard and offered free french fries for each ball returned.

Because proving that a product is actually dangerous can take precious time and provoke lawsuits from manufacturers, the CPSC occasionally uses a voluntary process to remove unsafe products more quickly. Under its fast-track process, which was first used in 1995, the CPSC gives product makers the chance to initiate their own recalls without facing a government order. This fast-track process takes an average of just nine days to produce a recall and allows companies to make the first move to address defects, which can protect their reputations among consumers.

There can be little doubt that the CPSC is making a major difference in preventing injuries and deaths from unsafe products. According to its own estimates, it saves the nation $10 billion a year in health care, property damage, and other costs that would have been spent without the CPSC's regulatory protection. In 2000 alone the agency recalled more 160 potentially hazardous products, and it issued new rules to reduce the risk of fires in upholstered furniture and to require that cigarette lighters be child resistant.

The CPSC is not the only agency involved in protecting consumers, however. As already noted, the federal government has a broad agenda that covers everything from tainted poultry to impure drinking water. Of all the agencies involved in that effort, few have a more important role than the Food and Drug Administration (FDA). By almost any measure, the FDA has an extraordinary mission. It is responsible for inspecting and overseeing the nearly 100,000 businesses that produce $1 trillion worth of regulated products, including food, prescription and over-the-counter medicines, medical devices such as artificial heart valves, radiation-emitting products such as microwave ovens, animal drugs and medicated feed, and cosmetics and toiletries.

The FDA is also responsible for protecting patients in clinical trials of medical products and drugs, reviewing the effectiveness of drugs and medical devices, monitoring the safety of new medical products after they enter the market, and assuring that all food and drug products are truthfully labeled. For example, the FDA requires that all food products carry nutrition labels indicating total calories, calories from fat, total carbohydrates, sodium, and a list of ingredients. In 1999 FDA proposed adding trans fatty acids to the list. According to its cost-benefit analysis, listing the artery-clogging fats on labels would prevent 6,400 cases of heart disease each year and 2,100 deaths.

America's food and drugs are safer today than they were even twenty years ago. In 1999 alone the FDA approved thirty-five new drugs for distribution, targeting diseases that cost society $600 billion a year in sickness and death, as well as approving new vaccines for Lyme disease and treatments for rheumatoid arthritis and an assortment of blood disorders. During the same year, the agency created a new test for detecting food-borne diseases, oversaw 200,000 inspections of retail businesses that sell tobacco products, recalled dozens of food products that it considered unsafe, and launched a new reporting initiative aimed at preventing 100,000 medical errors a year.

Like the CPSC, the FDA faces its own delicate balance in regulating food and drugs. On the one hand, the agency must make sure that each new drug is absolutely safe, which requires time-consuming testing. On the other hand, the agency must make sure that particularly effective drugs get to patients as fast as possible. Facing what it and its constituents saw as unacceptably long delays, the FDA began to accelerate the review process in the late 1990s, cutting the amount of time for review from almost three years for each new drug to just under a year and creating a fast-track process to expedite review of new drugs that are intended to treat a life-threatening disease or address a serious unmet medical need. One of the first drugs approved under the fast-track process was Herceptin, a genetically engineered treatment for fast-spreading breast cancer; it was approved in just under five months.

21 Expand Foreign Markets for U.S. Goods

The Founders believed in an economic policy of laissez-faire, a French term that simply means "to allow to do, to leave alone." Although they were quite willing to use early forms of economic penalties such as trade embargoes to protect the nation's fragile industries, the Founders wanted the economy to follow the natural laws of capitalism with little or no government involvement.

Much as they believed in capitalism, the Founders also understood that the new federal government would have to regulate at least some aspects of economic life. In 1816, for example, Congress placed a small tariff, or tax, on imported cloth, giving struggling New England textile manufacturers a slight economic advantage over foreign competitors. With the industry still struggling for survival against a flood of cheaper foreign goods, Congress raised the tariff again in both 1824 and 1828, producing a backlash among cotton growers in the South, who had developed a thriving export industry with foreign clothing makers.

When Congress raised the tariff a third time in 1832, the South Carolina legislature passed an "Ordinance of Nullification," declaring the tariffs of 1828 and 1832 null and void, forbidding collection of the tariff on South Carolina soil, and threatening to leave the Union if the tariff remained. The nation narrowly averted civil war when Congress promised to cut the tariff and South Carolina rescinded its nullification ordinance.

Many nations, including the United States, protect certain industries to this day through the use of import quotas (which restrict the amount of a particular product that can be purchased abroad) or export quotas (which restrict the amount of a product that can be sold to other nations), while occasionally imposing tariffs on particular imports to raise the price so that their own products are more attractive. Congress does not allow the export of technolo-

AP/WIDE WORLD/RICHARD VOGEL

The path to peace. Twenty years after the Vietnam War ended, consumer product giant General Electric became one of the first American corporations to start selling products in Vietnam. The federal government was partially responsible for opening the Vietnamese market to U.S. goods.

gies that can be used to build nuclear weapons, for example, and has long protected certain defense industries that would be essential should the nation ever be forced into another world war. Congress and the president have also used trade to promote human rights and democratic reform.

Despite occasional bouts of protectionism, Congress has generally acted to expand free trade over the past fifty years. Under the Trade Expansion Act of 1962, for example, Congress gave the president authority to cut tariffs by half and created the position now known as U.S. Trade Representative to act as a high-level presidential adviser and international negotiator on behalf of free trade. Congress extended the president's authority to lower tariffs twice over the next decade while also giving the president authority to battle unfair trading practices by other nations under the Trade and Tariff Act of 1984.

The two most important trade laws may be the two most recent, however. The first involved ratification of the North American Free Trade Agreement (NAFTA) in 1993. By removing all trade barriers between the United States, Mexico, and Canada, NAFTA created a single North American trading zone to compete with the European Union. Facing intense opposition from labor unions, which feared that high-paying U.S. jobs would migrate to low-paid Mexican workers, Congress provided financial relief for businesses and workers hurt by the agreement and authorized $1.5 billion for environmental cleanup along the U.S.-Mexican border.

The second and even more controversial law involved creation of the World Trade Organization (WTO) in 1994. As an international organization like the United Nations, the WTO acts as a forum for nations to resolve their disputes, which in this case involve trade.

The WTO is the direct descendant of the General Agreement on Tariffs and Trade (GATT), which had been formed at the end of World War II to reduce trade barriers among nations. Although GATT had largely succeeded over the years in reducing most tariffs on imports, it had made little progress in lowering more subtle barriers to trade such as government laws that restrict imports of seafood harvested with certain kinds of nets. Frustrated by the rising number of such indirect tariffs, the United States and 124 other nations met in 1994 to create the WTO.

Like GATT, the WTO had the broad authority to negotiate international trade agreements that would improve the free flow of goods and services. Unlike GATT, however, the WTO was given the power to enforce those agreements through a judicial process. The process begins when a nation files a complaint alleging that another nation has hampered free trade. If the complaint cannot be resolved through negotiation between the two countries, the complaint is turned over to a panel of trade experts who make a final ruling of guilt or innocence. Nations that are found guilty in this process have two choices: either change their practices or face retaliation by other WTO members.

This process has given individual nations considerable reason to lower the barriers to free trade. At the same time, however, the process has sparked a growing international protest movement involving three basic concerns.

First, the United States has criticized the WTO for making most of its decisions in secret. Unlike the U.S. legal system in which every defendant is guaranteed a public trial, the WTO is neither required to hold an open trial nor explain its final decision. As President Clinton complained in 1999, "The WTO has been treated for too long like some private priesthood for exports, where we know what's right and we pat you on the head and tell you to just go right along and play by the rules we reach."

Second, labor unions have protested that the WTO has done little to improve working conditions in other countries. To the contrary, labor unions suggest that the WTO has actually encouraged lower standards by lowering barriers to goods produced with cheap labor. The issue has also engaged many of America's colleges and universities, where students have organized boycotts of suppliers of Nike athletic wear made in Chinese sweatshops. In 1999, for example, the University of Notre Dame joined with Harvard and the University of California system to monitor working conditions in factories that produce clothing and other merchandise bearing their logos.

Third, environmental groups across the globe have joined to protest the WTO's resistance to standards on everything from endangered species to genetically altered foods. In 1996, for example, the WTO penalized the United States for demanding that Venezuela gasoline meet the Clean Air standards enacted by Congress. Two years later the WTO penalized the United States again for restricting imports of shrimp harvested with nets that can drown sea turtles. That same year the WTO punished European nations for limiting imports of U.S. beef treated with growth hormones.

Despite its considerable success in encouraging nations to reduce trade barriers, the WTO also reinforces other, less desirable national policies. Although Americans clearly benefit from the free flow of trade, they also lose one of their most effective tools for encouraging a cleaner, freer, more democratic world. The more the WTO and other international organizations punish the United States and other

Western nations for refusing to trade with countries that abuse human rights, deny basic freedoms, and add to the world's environmental crisis, the less willing the United States and its citizens may be to assert their demands for a better world.

22 Increase the Stability of Financial Institutions and Markets

The stock market crash of 1929 did more than devastate the American economy and produce the Great Depression. It also revealed deep problems with how stocks were sold to investors. Millions of new investors entered the stock market in the 1920s only to find out that the companies in which they had invested were virtually worthless.

Before 1934, when the Securities and Exchange Commission (SEC) was created, it was up to investors to determine whether a company was telling the truth about its stock. Since 1934 that responsibility has fallen to the SEC. Under the Securities Exchange Act of 1934 and a long list of subsequent laws, companies that offer their stock for sale to the public must tell the truth about their businesses, which means full disclosure of all financial statements as well as the stocks they are selling and the risks involved in investing. This information is to be contained in a detailed document called a prospectus.

At the same time, the act also required that anyone in the business of selling stocks, including brokers, dealers, and stock exchanges such as the New York Stock Exchange and Nasdaq, must treat investors fairly and honestly and put investors' interests first. That means, for example, that individuals who know about a new stock offering in advance or have other so-called inside information on events that might increase or decrease the value of a given stock are prohibited from using that information to benefit themselves.

To enforce that law, the SEC brings 400–500 cases a year against individuals and companies that violate the securities law. In 1998, for example, the SEC filed a complaint against a radio talk show host, Jerome M. Wenger, who promoted a stock on his radio program "The Next SuperStock" without telling listeners that he had

An insider trader on trial. Bond trader Michael Millken was indicted and convicted of insider trading after one of the most extensive fraud investigations in federal government history.

been given $75,000 in cash and stock in return for the endorsement. The endorsement constituted a breach of insider trading and led to Wenger's arrest and prosecution for fraud.

The SEC is also responsible for giving investors basic information about investing. Its road map to investing provides a host of information on navigating today's highly complicated stock market. The website includes all the basics, as well as detailed warnings to anyone thinking of becoming a day-trader—someone who uses high-powered software to buy and sell stocks minute-by-minute throughout the day. The SEC's advice is simple: *be prepared to suffer financial losses.*

The SEC has mostly succeeded in its basic mission of protecting investors. Even as the amount of stock held by the public has soared into the tens of trillions of dollars, America's stock markets have remained the safest and fairest in the world. Investors can have confidence that the information they get on the stocks they buy is accurate. The SEC cannot guarantee that any given investor will make money, but it does make sure that every investment starts honestly.

Unfortunately, as the $60 billion collapse of the energy-trading firm Enron in 2001 demonstrated, corporations and their auditors still need policing. Enron misled its investors through false profit-and-loss statements, hidden partnerships, and inflated forecasts of future growth. Furthermore, Enron's auditors at the accounting firm of Arthur Andersen signed off on those statements without solid proof that their client was telling the truth.

Congress has also been forced to rescue investors from its own legislation. Although the rescues have often been buried in federal tax laws, the largest rescue in modern history occurred in 1989 with a $100 billion bailout of several banks referred to as savings and loans. The rescue was driven by bad investments and questionable loans made by hundreds of savings and loan institutions in the 1980s, at least some of which were prompted by deregulation of the industry in 1978, 1980, and 1982.

Under the Depository Institutions Act of 1982, for example, savings and loans were given permission to diversify their investments and increase profits. The federal government removed its restrictions on interest ceilings on passbooks savings accounts and allowed savings and loans to put more of their money into commercial mortgages, loans, and property leases. As it turned out, many of those mortgages, loans, and leases were risky at best and worthless at worst. As the deregulation continued, so did the loosening of oversight by the Federal Home Loan Bank Board, which was responsible for guaranteeing that savings and loans made responsible investments.

As one savings and loan after another went under, the federal government was forced to pay out billions to cover empty savings accounts, each one of which was insured by the Federal Savings and Loan Insurance Corporation (FSLIC) for up to $100,000. By 1987 the FSLIC was $3.8 billion in debt. By 1988 more than 500 of the nation's nearly 3,200 savings and loans were insolvent, of which almost 200 were in the Southwest where oil prices had plummeted. With the industry losing as much as $20 million a day on bad investments by 1989, Congress enacted the Financial Institutions Reform, Recovery and Enforcement Act, which provided $50 billion in federal funds to close or sell off hundreds of failing savings and loans. Congress also reregulated the industry, first by restructuring the Federal Home Loan Bank Board to better monitor the savings and loan industry, and second by creating the Resolution Trust Corporation (RTC) to sell or restructure individual failing savings and loan banks.

23 Increase Arms Control and Disarmament

Having emerged victorious from World War II, the United States developed a new theory for how to contain the Soviet Union. Because the Soviet Union and its allies had a huge numerical advantage in armed forces, containment depended in part on the willingness of the United States to use its nuclear weapons to stop the spread of communism, even if that meant it would destroy itself in the process. Under this theory of deterrence, the United States had to convince the Soviet Union that it had the nuclear weapons to

Rest in peace. Retired B-52 bombers at a "boneyard" in Arizona. Nuclear disarmament began with a reduction in the number of missiles and bombers that could deliver weapons.

inflict massive damage and that it would not hesitate for a moment to use those weapons at the first hint of Soviet aggression.

The Soviet Union also adopted the theory, matching U.S. nuclear technology warhead for warhead over the decades. The resulting arms race, as it was called, eventually led to the theory of mutually assured destruction, or MAD. Knowing that each country would be destroyed in the event of nuclear war was seen as the essential fear that would prevent nuclear war from ever occurring. This fear did not prevent the two nations from building enough nuclear weapons and delivery systems—intercontinental ballistic missiles (ICBMs), submarine-launched ballistic missiles (SLBMs), and long-range nuclear bombers—to destroy the world many times over.

Even as the United States built its nuclear arsenal, it worked to reduce the spread of nuclear weapons and negotiate arms reductions. In 1955, for example, President Dwight Eisenhower met with Soviet Premier Nikita Khrushchev in Geneva, Switzerland, to lay the groundwork for a possible arms treaty. It was the first meeting between the leaders of the great superpowers since World War II, but it failed to produce an agreement on the president's "open skies" arms inspection treaty that would have allowed full inspection of each nation's nuclear weapons programs. Further negotiations came to an abrupt halt in May 1960 when the Soviets shot down a U.S. spy plane.

Despite these early failures, there were many successes over the years, including creation of the Arms Control and Disarmament Agency in 1961 to help presidents develop strategies for reducing arms, ratification of the Nuclear Test Ban Treaty of 1963, and ratification of the Nuclear Nonproliferation Treaty of 1969. Congress even adopted the Outer Space Treaty in 1967, which provides a set of core principles governing the peaceful uses of space that have been followed to this day. Under the treaty, which has been ratified or signed by 123 nations, the exploration and use of outer space is to be carried out for the benefit of humankind and free for exploration by all nations. Outer space is also to remain free of all weapons of mass destruction, including nuclear, chemical, and biological; astronauts are to be considered as envoys, or ambassadors, of humankind; and the moon and other celestial bodies cannot be claimed by any nation as its property or used as bases for military forces or nuclear testing. Finally, nations are liable for damage caused by their space objects, and space is not to be used as a dumping ground for waste. Although the treaty has worked well over the past thirty years, most nations do not yet have the technology to use space for any purposes, peaceful or not. It will almost surely be tested in coming decades as technology advances.

Along with these expressions of international cooperation, there have also been occasional breakthroughs in reducing the actual number of nuclear weapons. The first breakthrough occurred in 1972 with ratification of the Strategic Arms Limitation Treaty (SALT I) and the Anti-Ballistic Missile Treaty (ABM). Negotiations over the two treaties began in March 1967 under President Lyndon Johnson and continued under President Richard Nixon. Under SALT I the two superpowers agreed to freeze land-based missiles and nuclear submarine fleets at then existing levels. Under ABM the two nations also agreed not to deploy an extensive protective shield against nuclear attack. Together the two treaties guaranteed that both nations would continue to operate under mutually assured destruction.

Negotiations on a second arms reduction treaty, SALT II, began almost immediately after ratification of SALT I. By November 1974 the two nations appeared to have reached an historic agreement to ban the construction of any new land-based nuclear missile launchers, limit the deployment of new kinds of offensive arms, and limit the total number of nuclear bombers and missiles. Unfortunately, negotiators for President Gerald Ford and Soviet Premier Leonid Brezhnev could not reach an agreement on the total number of nuclear warheads those bombers and missiles could carry.

By the time the United States and Soviet Union finally reached an agreement on the number of warheads almost a decade later in 1990, the original SALT II treaty was long gone. Although President Jimmy Carter had submitted the SALT II to the Senate, it was withdrawn after the Soviet Union invaded Afghanistan in 1979. In 1980 Carter announced that the United States would comply with the treaty as long as the Soviet Union followed in kind.

By 1986, however, President Ronald Reagan concluded that the Soviet Union had failed to follow this framework of mutual restraint, and therefore the United States would no longer follow the outlines of the treaty. Even though he also announced that the United States did not anticipate any substantial growth in its nuclear arsenal, Congress had already provided the funding he had requested for research on the Strategic Defense Initiative, a space-based shield against nuclear weapons. In doing so, Congress and the president signaled the nation's readiness to abandon the ABM treaty.

With the Soviet Union well on the way to collapse by 1989, when the Berlin Wall was torn down, negotiations between the United States and Russia began anew and soon produced a second breakthrough. Under the Strategic Arms Reduction Treaty (START) of 1991, which was signed by President George H. W. Bush and Soviet President Mikhail Gorbachev, the two nations agreed to reduce their missiles and bombers to no more than 1,600 each and their nuclear warheads to no more than 6,000 each. Both goals were not only met by the December

5, 2001, deadline but were actually exceeded. In May 2002 the United States and Russia signed an agreement to reduce their nuclear warheads by two-thirds, to no more than 2,200 each by 2012.

However, the future of arms control is not likely to involve intricate negotiations between current and former superpowers. Rather, it will focus on limiting the number of other nations that develop nuclear weapons. This diffuse nuclear proliferation can create what foreign policy experts describe as a chain-reaction arms race that can make the use of single weapons much more likely than ever before. Experts believe that as many as forty nations now have the economic and technological capacity to become nuclear powers. And at least four—North Korea, Israel, India, and Pakistan—have the capability to launch those weapons with short- and even intermediate-range missiles.

24 Protect the Wilderness

The federal effort to protect the nation's remaining wilderness actually began with a public interest group called the Wilderness Society. Created in 1935, the society was and still is dedicated to ensuring that "future generations will enjoy the clean air and water, wildlife, beauty and opportunities for recreation and renewal that pristine forests, rivers, deserts and mountains provide." To achieve that mission, the society drafted a law in 1955 to set aside some of the nation's remaining wilderness from further development. The core of the bill was the following definition of wilderness: "A wilderness, in contrast with those areas where man and his works dominate the landscape, is hereby recognized as an area where the earth and its community of life are untrammeled by man, where man himself is a visitor who does not remain."

The draft hardly inspired immediate enthusiasm. Colorado representative Wayne Aspinall called it "a crazy idea," and the National Park Service opposed it. However, nine years later the bill became law because what it did inspire was public support. The nation had been moving toward greater support for wilderness protection since

©DAVID MUENCH

Worth preserving. The Kings River in Kings Canyon, California, is one of 31 rivers in 13 states stretching a total of nearly 2,400 miles that are protected as part of the Wild and Scenic Rivers system.

the early 1950s when the federal government had sought to build a dam within the Dinosaur National Monument in Utah. The speaker of the House, Texas Democrat Sam Rayburn, said that he had received more mail about that one dam than on any other subject that year.

Despite this growing public support, the legislation was stalled by the logging, agriculture, and mining industries, all of which wanted access to the wilderness. Moreover, the Eisenhower administration believed that environmental issues were distinctly local concerns, noting at one point that "water pollution is a uniquely local blight. Primary responsibility for solving the problem lies not with the federal government but rather must be assumed and exercised, as it has been, by state and local governments."

Unwilling to let a perfect bill become the enemy of a good or even mediocre one, and hoping for future expansion, advocates of protection finally settled on a compromise Wilderness Act in 1964. Under the initial law, the federal government assumed responsibility for protecting 9 million acres of wilderness, and under its subsequent amendments, the federal government set a number of boundaries on who and what could enter the wilderness and how. Humans can enter wilderness areas, for example, but only on foot, on horseback, or by nonmotorized boats such as canoes. Mechanized access is not allowed, meaning that mountain bikes and all-terrain vehicles are not allowed. Livestock grazing is allowed, but mining is only permissible on preexisting claims, and no development of dams, reservoirs, or power lines is allowed. With steady expansion over the decades, the Wilderness Act now protects over 100 million acres of land, including 57 million acres protected under the Alaska Land Protection Act of 1980.

Even as Congress moved forward on wilderness protection, it rejected early calls for a scenic rivers system. The Johnson administration started in 1965 with a simple proposal for a wild rivers system composed of portions of just six rivers: the Salmon and Clearwater in Idaho, the Green in Wyoming, the Rogue in Oregon, the Rio Grande in New Mexico, and the Suwannee in Georgia and Florida. The draft legislation prohibited construction of any dams on the rivers and proposed further study on possible inclusion of nine other rivers for protection. After removing the Green and Suwannee Rivers and adding the Eleven Point in Missouri and the Cacapon and Shenandoah in West Virginia, the Senate passed the bill in 1966. But the House resisted, and the bill died without action.

The Senate and White House were undeterred, however, and brought the bill back in the next Congress. Facing growing pressure from the same public interest groups that had propelled the Wilderness Act, Congress finally passed the Wild and Scenic Rivers Act in 1968, providing for the designation and preservation of rivers with what Congress called "outstandingly remarkable scenic, recreational, geologic, fish and wildlife, historic, cultural, or other similar values."

Under the act and its later amendments, a river can be protected either through an act of Congress or through designation by the Department of the Interior as one of three different kinds of rivers in the National Wild and Scenic Rivers System: wild river areas that are generally inaccessible except by trail, scenic rivers that have shorelines that are largely primitive but accessible in places by road, and recreational rivers that have some development but can still be protected. The law requires a buffer zone between a designated river and any development such as housing, hotels, or recreation.

Every president since Lyndon Johnson has added at least one river to the wild rivers system. In 1992, for example, the first president Bush added 32 miles to the system when he signed the Arkansas Wild and Scenic Rivers Act protecting 16.5 miles of Richland Creek and 15.8 miles of the Buffalo River near Fallsville. Just over 9 miles of the Buffalo River were designated as scenic and another 6 miles as wild. In 2000 President Clinton added another 255 miles to the system when he signed the Lower Delaware Wild and Scenic Rivers Act and the White Clay Creek Wild and Scenic Rivers System Act. By the time the second president Bush arrived in office, almost 11,300 miles of 160 wild, scenic, and recreational rivers had been incorporated into the National Wild and Scenic Rivers System.

25 Promote Space Exploration

"I believe this nation should commit itself to achieving the goal, before this decade is out, of landing a man on the moon and returning him safely to the Earth." That is how President John F. Kennedy announced the Apollo program in May 1961.

In doing so, Kennedy used the powers of the presidency to commit the nation to a nearly impossible task. As commander in chief, he mobilized the U.S. military to make its knowledge of missile sys-

NASA

Fixing the Hubble Space Telescope. Launched in 1990, the Hubble Space Telescope orbits 375 miles and can see to the edge of the solar system. The only way to fix the telescope is to put engineers into orbit with it.

tems available for the Apollo program. (It was a huge Titan missile that hurled the first astronauts into orbit). As diplomat in chief, he persuaded other nations to allow the United States to build tracking systems to monitor the first space flights. As administrator in chief, he oversaw the creation of the National Aeronautics and Space Administration as it developed the technology and designed, tested, and built the equipment needed to send a man to the moon. Kennedy also convinced Congress to make the huge financial investments required to make the Apollo program a reality.

The United States reached Kennedy's goal with five months to spare when members of the crew of Apollo 11 planted the American flag on the moon on July 20, 1969. The astronauts also left a plaque that read, "Here men from planet Earth first set foot upon the Moon, July 1969 A.D. We came in peace for all mankind."

The moon landing was a herculean effort that grew exponentially over time. In 1962 the National Aeronautics and Space Administration employed 23,000 government workers and a handful of scientists who worked under contract for the agency. By 1965 NASA had grown to 32,000 government employees and roughly 80,000 contract scientists, not to mention another 100,000–200,000 workers who were busy building the rockets that would carry Neil Armstrong, Michael Collins, and Edwin "Buzz" Aldrin Jr. to the moon and back.

The Apollo program was about much more than just sending a man to the moon safely, however. It was also about keeping up with the Soviet Union in the space race and thus counter what Kennedy and his successors saw as a clear threat to U.S. security. The Soviets had been first into space with a satellite called Sputnik in 1957; first into space with a live animal, a dog named Laika, in 1959; and first into space with a human being, Yuri Gagarin, in 1961.

That Kennedy's goal was nearly impossible was obvious. NASA had to design, test, and build three different spacecraft in under six years, the first of which carried the first U.S. astronaut, John Glenn, into earth orbit in 1962. Along the way the space program generated new technologies that helped strengthen the U.S. economy, not to mention new consumer products such as Velcro and Tang.

The endeavor was fraught with risk. Although all of the astronauts launched into space miraculously made it back to Earth alive, the first three Apollo astronauts lost their lives in a disastrous fire on the launch pad in 1967, and one of the last Apollo missions barely made it home after a liquid oxygen tank exploded en route to the moon. (Ron Howard made an Academy Award–winning movie about that near-disaster, called *Apollo 13*.) The risks make the ultimate success that much more impressive.

Landing a man on the moon was not the only goal of the U.S. space program, however. Not only has Congress continued to support human exploration of space, it has also invested heavily in space science, which inquires about how the universe began, and earth science, which investigates global warming and the ozone layer that protects earth from ultraviolet radiation.

NASA's space scientists do their work by sending deep probes into space from earth and by staring into deep space from just above earth through the Hubble Space Telescope. Over the years the world has seen Venus up close thanks to the Magellan mission, Jupiter and Uranus courtesy of Galileo, and Saturn courtesy of Voyager. The world has also seen the edge of the universe through the huge lens of the Hubble Space Telescope.

NASA's earth scientists do their work in the opposite direction, by looking at earth from space, whether through the portals of the space shuttle or through a ring of satellites orbiting the earth. NASA researchers are studying a host of questions affecting the future of the environment, from the impact of ozone depletion on cancer rates to the role of forest fires in global warming to the relationship between climate and the outbreak of diseases such as the West Nile virus. NASA's next major earth science mission is Project Aqua, which will orbit the earth every sixteen days for six years. The mission will provide a running chronology of how earth behaves by providing data on the world's temperature, humidity, clouds, precipitation, snow and sea ice, sea temperature, soil moisture, and overall climate.

Finally, NASA's human exploration scientists plan to do their work through the new international space station, which opened for business in 2000 but awaits final outfitting of its six laboratories.

NASA will continue to ferry equipment, supplies, and personnel to the station via the reusable space shuttle.

NASA has undergone its share of challenges along with its successes. With the Apollo mission over and the federal budget deficit rising, the United States decided to create a reusable launch system built around the space shuttle to propel cargo into orbit. Despite its promised reliability, the "space truck," as it became known, was plagued by cost increases, breakdowns, design flaws, and launch delays, all of which contributed to the 1986 Challenger catastrophe that killed all seven crew members, including America's first teacher in space, Christa McAuliffe. The streak of bad luck returned in 1999 when two probes to Mars were lost just before reaching their destination. More recently, the international space station has been cut back to control its rapidly rising costs. Originally priced at $8 billion, the project has been cut back several times, yet may end up costing $30 billion or more.

CONCLUSION

This detailed history of government achievement reveals important lessons for finding a clear pathway to success for recent efforts to restore homeland security, conquer new diseases, master the global economy, and battle terrorism. The first lesson is that government, like all institutions, rarely gets it perfect on the first try. Government's greatest achievements have involved bursts of significant legislative activity, followed by intense administrative effort, followed in turn by bursts of expanded authority. Except for rebuilding Europe after World War II, which was a success within four years of its launch, the rest of government's greatest endeavors have involved sporadic expansion of the kind witnessed in environmental protection. Simply stated, government learns over time, often returning to the same statute over and over to fix past mistakes, cover new problems, and adjust to changes in society.

The second lesson is that the federal government needs strong civic and private partners to succeed. It is hard to imagine how the federal government could have made progress on civil rights without a host of nonprofit partners, including the National Association for the Advancement of Colored People and the National Organization for Women; how it could have improved workplace protection without the help of labor unions and private businesses; how it could have expanded international trade without the help of trade associations such as the National Association of Manufacturers, Chamber of Commerce, or National Federation of Independent Businesses; or how it could have succeeded in reducing poverty among older Americans without the National Council of Senior Citizens or the AARP.

The third lesson is that the federal government simply does not have enough employees to do everything. Just as it is impossible to imagine success without civic and private partners, it is also impossible to imagine how 1.8 million federal civil servants could have implemented all the laws described above without the help of the 4.6 million people who work indirectly for the federal government under mandates to state and local government, the 11 million non-profit workers who make up the civic infrastructure that does so much in lieu of government, or the 6 million federal contractors and more than 2.5 million federal grantees who do much of the heavy lifting on behalf of Congress and the president.

Finally, Congress and the president have often relied on the federal courts to spark public demand for action, enforce the laws, and call the nation to the greater good. It was not Congress that acted first on breaking down the color barrier in public accommodations but the Supreme Court, not the president who made the major decisions implementing the Americans with Disabilities Act but the federal courts.

As noted earlier, laws are not self-enforcing. They must be administered by people, enforced by people, and obeyed by people. Audacious goals demand an audacious society, one ready to take risks, embrace change, and imagine a better future. Courage, creativity, endurance, and love of country and community simply cannot be legislated. They are part of the national character that makes government's greatest achievements possible. Governments do not dream, people do.

3

Facing the Future

*Greatest Priorities of the
Next Half-Century*

No one can be sure what the next fifty years will hold by way of government achievement, nor can anyone be sure just what the federal government will be doing fifty years from now. The federal government will almost certainly launch new endeavors, some of which will be driven by scientific breakthroughs already under way, others of which will emerge from tragedies yet to unfold. Just as the events of September 11 spawned an entirely new effort to protect homeland security, events of some future September may also spark new government initiative.

If the past is prologue, however, government will continue with many of its greatest endeavors of the past fifty years. The federal government has been working to protect workers, help veterans readjust, defend the nation, build roads, enhance transportation, connect communities, promote economic growth, and support the poor for a quarter of a millennium. It is hardly likely to stop now. Each generation has left its mark on these endeavors, often by expanding coverage of existing programs to entirely new populations or by tearing down new barriers to old rights.

Government certainly still has work to do to honor promises made in the past. Only two of the government's fifty greatest endeavors of the past fifty years have been completed: rebuilding Europe after World War II and driving the Iraqis out of Kuwait in the 1991 Persian Gulf war. The rest of the fifty greatest endeavors are still active. Some are likely to grow more intense over the coming years in response to new threats such as terrorism, global warming, or diseases such as HIV-AIDS. Others are likely to require new investments to prevent past gains from being undermined by deteriorating "infrastructure," whether it be antiquated voting machines, rusting highway bridges, or aging classrooms. Still others have yet to achieve minimal success. The cold war with the Soviet Union may be over, but billions of people still live under totalitarian regimes, terrorism threatens to split the world by region and religion, and U.S. humanitarian aid continues to lag well behind international need.

THE NATURE OF SUCCESS AND FAILURE

Proud as they might be of what the federal government tried to accomplish these past fifty years, Americans rarely let that pride obscure the reality that government did not succeed at every endeavor it launched. Asked in 1998 to rate the federal government's performance on eight separate endeavors, a majority of Americans said that government had done only a fair or poor job on seven: reducing juvenile delinquency, reducing poverty, ensuring that every American has access to affordable health care, ensuring that all Americans can afford to send their children to college, setting academic standards for the schools, providing a decent standard of living for the elderly, and conserving the nation's natural resources.[1] Ensuring safe food and drugs was the only endeavor where a majority of Americans said government had done either a good or excellent job.

1. Pew Research Center for the People and the Press, *Deconstructing Distrust: How Americans View Their Government* (Washington, 1998).

Yet even as they criticized government's performance, Americans clearly distinguished between two types of poor performance: one rooted in the nature of the problem, the other in government's own weakness. Thus, of the 84 percent who said the federal government had done a fair or poor job reducing poverty, only 28 percent said the failure was government's fault compared to 51 percent who said the issue was just too difficult and complex. Conversely, of the 74 percent who said the federal government had done a fair or poor job in setting academic standards for the schools, 39 percent said the failure was the government's fault compared to 33 percent who said the issue was too difficult or complex.

Americans were more likely to blame government for the poor performance on three of the eight issues (setting academic standards, ensuring affordable health care, and conserving the environment). They were more likely to blame inherent difficulty for poor performance on the government's four other failing efforts (providing a decent standard of living for the elderly, providing access to college, reducing juvenile delinquency, and reducing poverty).

Types of Failure

The 450 historians and political scientists who rated the government's fifty greatest endeavors of the past half-century in 2000 also seemed to distinguish between two types of failures, one rooted in the government's inability to solve a difficult problem and the other in government's inability to solve an easy problem. Government can tackle a difficult problem and fail, thereby producing an understandable failure, or tackle an easy problem and fail, producing an unacceptable failure. It is one thing to fail a hard course such as organic chemistry but quite another to fail a gut course such as physics for poets.

The fact that these problems were tough does not make the lack of success any less troubling, however, nor does difficulty alone explain the failure. The United States could have been much more successful advancing human rights and providing humanitarian aid, for example, had it invested more money in foreign aid. Measured in

Most Understandable Failures of the Past Half-Century[a]

Overall rank	Endeavor	Ranking based on		
		Difficulty	Success	Distance
1	Advance human rights and provide humanitarian relief	1	47	−46
2	Develop and renew impoverished communities	4	49	−45
3	Increase arms control and disarmament	2	35	−33
4 tie	Reduce crime	6	42	−36
	Improve mass transportation	10	46	−36
5	Reform welfare	8	43	−35
6	Improve elementary and secondary education	13	44	−31
7	Improve government performance	22	48	−26
8	Increase international economic development	9	33	−24
9 tie	Control immigration	15	37	−22
	Increase health care access for low-income families	16	38	−22

a. This ranking is based on a comparison of the difficulty of a given endeavor and the government's ultimate success. In theory, failure on a very difficult problem, such as advancing human rights, is more tolerable than failure on an easy problem. In theory again, the most difficult problem should be the least successful. This table was constructed by taking the twenty-five most difficult endeavors and subtracting each one's ranking on success to generate the distance between difficulty and success. The greater the negative value is, the more understandable the failure.

absolute terms, the United States has long been one of the world's most generous nations, spending more than $10 billion a year. But measured by what it could have contributed given the size of its economy, the United States has spent much less than it could have, trailing most other Western democracies in helping poor nations.

The United States also could have put more energy into developing poor communities, promoting urban mass transit, improving elementary and secondary education, and increasing health care access for low-income families, whether through increased spending or further mandates to the states. There are trade-offs in such choices, of course. Greater federal spending in the war on poverty or

Least Acceptable Failures of the Past Half-Century[a]

Overall rank	Endeavor	Ranking based on Difficulty	Success	Distance
1	Increase the supply of low-income housing	26	50	−24
2	Expand job training and placement	33	45	−8

a. This ranking is based on a comparison of the difficulty of a given endeavor and the government's ultimate success. In theory, failure on an easy problem, such as increasing the supply of low-income housing, is less acceptable than failure on a difficult problem. In theory again, the easiest problem should be the most successful. This table was constructed by taking the twenty-five least difficult endeavors and subtracting each one's ranking on success to generate the distance between difficulty and success. The greater the negative value is, the less understandable the failure.

new mandates to the states on elementary and secondary education might have created problems affecting other endeavors on the list of government's greatest achievements—for example, weakening the prospects for successfully reducing the federal budget deficit or increasing public demand for deregulation.

Ease is no guarantee of success, however. The United States easily could have increased the supply of low-income housing and enhanced job training and placement by injecting relatively small amounts of money into the effort. Both efforts have been plagued by public disquiet and bureaucratic scandal, suggesting that the historians and political scientists were measuring the pure difficulty of an issue, not its political or administrative impossibility. The United States also could have reformed taxes by merely simplifying the tax code, but Congress simply did not have the will to do so, perhaps because of the relentless lobbying by interest groups that preferred the protection of complexity.

Types of Success

There are also at least two kinds of success. Government can tackle a very difficult issue and succeed, creating a remarkable success, or tackle a very easy issue and succeed, producing an easy success.

Most Remarkable Successes of the Past Half-Century[a]

Overall rank	Endeavor	Ranking based on		
		Difficulty	Success	Distance
1	Contain communism	5	4	41
2	Reduce the federal budget deficit	7	6	37
3	Rebuild Europe after World War II	14	1	35
4	Promote equal access to public accommodations	12	5	33
5	Expand the right to vote	19	2	29
6	Reduce workplace discrimination	3	20	27
7	Promote space exploration	17	13	20
8	Reduce disease	23	11	16
9	Improve air quality	11	28	11
10	Improve water quality	21	26	3

a. This ranking is based on a comparison of the difficulty of a given endeavor and the government's ultimate success. In theory, success on a difficult problem, such as containing communism, is more admirable than success on an easy problem. This table was constructed by taking the twenty-five most difficult endeavors and subtracting each one's ranking on success to generate the distance between difficulty and success. The greater the positive value is, the more remarkable the success.

Again, it is one thing to ace a basic course, quite another to pass an honors seminar.

Just as ease is no guarantee of success, difficulty is no guarantee of failure. Containing communism, reducing workplace discrimination or the federal budget deficit, promoting equal access to public accommodations, rebuilding Europe after World War II, promoting space exploration, and expanding the right to vote were all rated as both difficult and successful. At least for these endeavors, where there was a will to tackle a difficult problem, there appeared to be a way to achieve.

Just because some endeavors were easy does not make them trivial. Four of the ten easiest successes were among the twenty-five most important endeavors, including ensuring safe food and drinking water, which was rated the eighth most important problem the federal government tried to solve over the past fifty years. Moreover, it is also not clear that most Americans, let alone their interest groups, would have tolerated anything other than action on helping veterans

Easiest Successes of the Past Half-Century[a]

Overall rank	Endeavor	Ranking based on		
		Difficulty	Success	Distance
1	Strengthen the nation's highway system	49	3	4
2	Support veterans' readjustment and training	48	7	9
3	Expand homeownership	50	15	15
4	Promote scientific and technological research	47	14	17
5	Increase access to postsecondary education	46	17	21
6	Strengthen the national defense	44	8	14
7	Promote financial security in retirement	38	10	22
8	Increase health care access for older Americans	31	9	28
9	Ensure safe food and drinking water	36	18	32
10	Enhance consumer protection	32	23	41

a. This ranking is based on a comparison of the difficulty of a given endeavor and the government's ultimate success. In theory, success on an easy problem, such as strengthening the nation's highway system, is less admirable than success on a difficult problem. This table was constructed by taking the twenty-five least difficult endeavors and subtracting each one's ranking on success to generate the distance between difficulty and success. The smaller the positive value is, the less surprising the success.

readjust to life after war, building the interstate highway system, or promoting homeownership.

SETTING PRIORITIES FOR THE NEXT HALF-CENTURY

At least some of the government's greatest priorities of the next fifty years originate in its greatest disappointments of the past. Having fallen short on important, tough problems such as advancing human rights abroad, renewing poor communities, and reducing nuclear arms, perhaps the federal government should work harder.

Yet setting priorities is not just about addressing past failures. It is also about protecting past achievements. It could be, for example, that advancing human rights abroad would cost so much in time, energy, and federal dollars that the federal government would be

Next steps in nuclear disarmament. Two Titan nose cones await their destruction as part of the arms control process. Having reduced the number of missiles and bombers, the United States and Soviet Union finally agreed in 1991 to reduce the number of warheads.

unable to maintain the same level of support for expanding voting rights, improving water quality, or promoting financial security in retirement.

Moreover, government success can ebb and flow with changing economic, social, and political circumstances. It also changes with events such as September 11, the Florida election impasse, or the anthrax scare, all of which exposed problems in past endeavors. Success also changes with sudden and unexpected breakthroughs such as the May 2002 agreement to cut nuclear weapons by more than half over the next decade.

If perseverance is one source of achievement, then government success also changes with the mere passage of time. The 1996 Welfare Reform Act was looking very successful in its first four years, for example. Poverty rates among all demographic groups declined for their seventh year in a row in 2000, with the child poverty rate reaching its lowest level since 1976, largely because welfare recipients were required to work under the 1996 reforms. Whether that achievement proves ephemeral may well depend on the economy, which entered an economic downturn in March 2001, thereby reducing the number of jobs that welfare recipients can take.

Updating the List of Endeavors

The first step in rating government's greatest priorities of the future is to update the list of government's greatest endeavors of the past. Rebuilding Europe after World War II and maintaining stability in the Persian Gulf were both removed from the list of potential priorities because they were no longer active by 2001, making room for the next two active endeavors in line: helping victims of disaster and reducing illegal drug use.

Help Victims of Disaster   The federal government has been sharing risks, preventing natural and human-made disasters, and helping victims recover since 1950 when Congress provided low-interest loans to help citizens rebuild homes and businesses in the wake of hurricanes, tornadoes, blizzards, and floods. Congress later created a new flood insurance and prevention program, provided funding for fire and chemical accident research, and created the Federal Emergency Management Agency in 1979 as an administrative hub for coordinating relief.

Reduce Illegal Drug Use   The federal government has been regulating illegal drugs since at least 1919 when the Treasury Department's Bureau of Alcohol, Firearms, and Tobacco was put in charge of enforcing the Eighteenth Amendment, which prohibited the sale or consumption of alcohol. Although the Eighteenth Amendment was repealed under the Twenty-First Amendment fourteen years later, Congress continues to regulate illegal drugs and encourage treatment through a number of statutes, including the Drug Abuse Control Act of 1968, creation of the Drug Enforcement Administration in 1973, and the Anti-Drug Abuse Acts of 1986 and 1988.

Updating Names

Several endeavors were renamed to reflect contemporary realities. "Reform welfare" became "reduce dependency among welfare recipients" to acknowledge the federal government's current welfare-to-work focus. "Contain communism" became "promote and protect democracy" to recognize the end of the cold war. "Reduce the federal budget deficit" became "balance the federal budget" to emphasize what now appears to have been a momentary success in actually achieving a balanced budget. Finally, "expand the right to vote" was changed to "expand and protect the right to vote" to reflect past gains and contemporary threats.

Absent: Homeland Defense

As if to demonstrate the role of crisis in setting new priorities, homeland defense was not included when the list of government's most intensive endeavors of the present was created. This is not to suggest that terrorism was not on the federal agenda before September 11. The United States most certainly knew about Osama bin Laden and his al-Qaida network before September—indeed, the Federal Bureau of Investigation had him listed as America's most wanted criminal since 1998. Nor does it suggest that no one had warned of the potential for terrorist attacks on U.S. soil. Almost two years to the day before the attacks on New York and Washington, the U.S. Commission on National Security in the 21st Century predicted that someday soon "Americans will likely die on American soil, possibly in large numbers." Rather, no one could or did anticipate the extraordinary sophistication and cruelty involved in the events of September 11 nor the extraordinary increase in federal effort required by the new war on terrorism.

Expanding the Sample Group

With this revised list of potential priorities in hand, a new combined sample of academics was drawn from among the 15,000 members of the American Historical Association, the 13,500 members of the American Political Science Association, the 13,000 members of the American Sociological Association, and the 22,000 members of the American Economic Association. The result was a list of 2,004 academics who specialize in either modern American history, American government, social policy, or public policy.

These are hardly the only experts who could have been asked about government's priorities, of course. One could have interviewed reporters, lawyers, scientists and engineers, judges, members of Congress, students in American history and government classes, or a host of other experts. What makes these academics valuable is that they are the ones who are in the nation's college classrooms teaching the next generation of reporters, lawyers, scientists and engineers, and so forth. To the extent one wants to know what students are learning about the past, present, and future of government's greatest endeavors, these are the academics to ask. Moreover, these are the academics most likely to have the training to know what government did in the past, which is central to the discussion of priorities for the future.

These academics were contacted by letter in July 2001 and given a password-protected website address where they could fill out the questionnaire on government's greatest priorities of the next fifty years. Respondents were first asked whether the federal government should be involved in each of the fifty current endeavors. If they answered "yes," respondents were then asked whether the federal government should be involved (1) because the endeavor concerns a very, somewhat, or not too important issue and (2) because the federal government has a large, moderate, or small responsibility to address the issue. They were also asked to choose whether the endeavor should be a top, a major, or a minor priority. These evaluations of each endeavor are shown in appendix C. However, if respondents answered "no," they were asked whether the federal government should not be involved (1) because the endeavor does not involve an important issue, (2) because the endeavor is not a federal responsibility, and (3) because past efforts to solve the problem have failed.

WILLIAM BRADSTREET/FOLIO

Worried about the future. As health care costs rose with inflation in the 1990s, so did fear of Medicare cuts and pressure for new benefits such as prescription drug coverage.

All totaled, 550 historians, political scientists, sociologists, and economists filled out the survey, producing a response rate of 27 percent.[2] This response rate was lower than the earlier mail survey of historians and political scientists for two likely reasons. First, the survey was done by Internet, rather than by mail, meaning that respondents could not take the survey unless they were online. Second, respondents were invited to complete the survey between August and October. Some respondents simply may have lost interest in completing the survey after September 11.

2. As with the first survey of historians and political scientists, results from this survey have a margin of error of ±5 percent, meaning that the true result among all historians and political scientists could vary by 5 percentage points in either direction of the reported answers. The survey was administered and tabulated by Princeton Survey Research Associates, a nationally recognized opinion research firm.

As with the first sample of just historians and political scientists, this second sample of 115 historians, 160 political scientists, 115 sociologists, and 160 economists is not remotely representative of the American public as a whole. As before, most respondents had a Ph.D., just under half had tenure at their college or university, most were white (89 percent), male (76 percent), self-identified liberals (58 percent), and Democrats (77 percent).

As before, however, this is the face of the faculty that has so much influence over the direction of government's greatest priorities through their teaching, research, and service. Moreover, as with the first sample of historians and political scientists, a sample more representative of the American public as a whole would not have reached radically different positions on what the federal government should or should not do in the future.

In addition, all of the percentages were adjusted to make sure that no one discipline was given more of a voice due to higher response rates.

To Be Continued

Prioritizing government's fifty greatest endeavors of today involves at least four decisions: which endeavors should be continued or stopped, which are most important, which are the federal government's greatest responsibility, and which should have the highest priority? An endeavor cannot be a top priority, or a priority of any kind, if it is not worth pursuing at all. Measured by their support for federal involvement, a majority of the 550 historians, political scientists, sociologists, and economists actually said the federal government should be involved in all fifty endeavors. Twenty-nine of the fifty endeavors were endorsed by at least 90 percent of the academics; another ten were endorsed by at least 80 percent; four, by at least 70 percent; another four, by at least 60 percent; and three, by at least 50 percent. Even the lowest ranking endeavor on the "continued" list—devolve responsibility to the states—was endorsed by 54 percent of respondents. These academics clearly had an appetite for endeavor.

Top Endeavors Government Should Continue in the Next Half-Century

Endeavor	Percent[a]
Improve air quality	98
Increase arms control and disarmament	97
Reduce disease	97
Ensure safe food and drinking water	97
Strengthen the nation's airways system	96
Improve water quality	96
Make government more transparent to the public	96
Enhance consumer protection	96
Protect the wilderness	96
Reduce exposure to hazardous waste	95
Expand and protect the right to vote	95

a. Respondents stating government involvement should continue.

The events of September 11 had almost no impact on the list of items to be continued but did have a very significant impact on the list of items to be abandoned. Academics responding after September 11 were significantly *more* likely to say the federal government should stop its efforts to devolve responsibility to the states (49 percent after September 11 versus 37 percent before), reform taxes (41 percent versus 32 percent, respectively), and increase market competition (40 percent versus 31 percent, respectively), and significantly *less* likely to say the federal government should stop its efforts to expand homeownership (30 percent after September 11 versus 40 percent before) and increase the supply of low-income housing (21 percent versus 32 percent, respectively). Although one cannot be sure whether respondents were thinking about the victims of the September attacks, the events clearly emphasized the need for a strong national government and higher spending while also demonstrating the necessity for government to help the needy.

Interestingly, respondents were statistically as likely to reject the effort to promote and protect democracy both before and after September 11. Respondents were not just reacting to the broad goal of the endeavor but to the fact that the endeavor was designed to

Endeavors Government Should Stop Pursuing Today

Endeavor	Percent[a]
Devolve responsibility to the states	46
Promote and protect democracy	45
Stabilize agricultural prices	41
Reduce illegal drug use	39
Reform taxes	39
Increase market competition	37
Expand homeownership	33
Increase the supply of low-income housing	24
Reduce dependency among welfare recipients	24
Expand job training and placement	22

a. Respondents stating endeavor should be discontinued.

impede communism. Some respondents may have ranked it low on future involvement because the cold war is over and communism seems in broad decline, whereas others may have been focusing on the Vietnam War as an example of a particular failure. Noble as protecting democracy seems as a broad goal, federal action has included its share of what these respondents saw as uncertain goals and mixed success. Of the respondents who said the endeavor should be discontinued, 55 percent said it was not an important issue, 47 percent said past policies had failed, and just 29 percent said it was not a federal responsibility.

Although there were differences within the ratings by discipline and demographics, almost all of the variation can be explained by ideology. Liberals were more likely than conservatives to endorse continuation for thirty-four of the fifty endeavors, while conservatives were more likely than liberals to endorse continuation for just seven.

There were no surprises among the endeavors each group favored. Conservatives were more likely than liberals to endorse devolving responsibilities to the states (91 percent versus 37 percent), reform taxes (96 percent versus 48 percent), and increasing market competition (89 percent versus 51 percent). Liberals were more likely than conservatives to favor renewing impoverished communities (92 percent versus 34 percent), expanding job training (91 percent versus 30 percent), and improving mass transportation (96 percent versus 48 percent). Ideology also helps explain the differences among the academic disciplines. The fact that 63 percent of the economists rated themselves as conservative or moderate, compared to 45 percent of the historians, 37 percent of the political scientists, and just 19 percent of the sociologists, clearly explains why economists generally gave lower endorsements to almost all of the fifty endeavors than did the historians, political scientists, and sociologists For example, just 45 percent of economists said government should continue the effort to expand homeownership and just 32 percent supported continued stabilization of agricultural prices. Ideology also helps explain why sociologists gave higher endorsements to more of the endeavors than historians, political scientists, and economists.

Demography helps explain some of the differences between the disciplines, too. The economists were much more likely to be male than the sociologists. A third of the sociologists were female, compared to a quarter of the historians and just under a fifth of the economists and political scientists. Economics may be a discipline that draws somewhat more conservative individuals by nature, but it also seems to attract individuals who are more likely to be conservative by gender.

Despite these differences the rankings would not have changed had the sample been more representative of the American public as a whole. Although levels of support would have dropped here and risen there, the fact is that most of the respondents—liberal, moderate, or conservative—favored continuation of most of the endeavors and in mostly the same order. Although a sample composed solely of conservatives or liberals would have produced different rankings, the American public actually splits roughly equally into conservative, moderate, and liberal affinities. In this regard the economists come closest to representing the American public as a whole, at 34 percent liberal, 49 percent moderate, and 14 percent conservative. Adding more conservatives to their midst would have altered the list only slightly.

Degrees of Importance

Once past the threshold question of whether the federal government should continue or discontinue each endeavor, setting priorities involves a more basic assessment of importance. In theory, the federal government's greatest priorities should involve the nation's most important problems.

The list of important endeavors combines a mix of past successes and disappointments. These respondents believe that the federal government still has important work to do on voting rights, retirement security, air quality, and ensuring safe food and drinking water, all of which made the list of government's greatest achievements of the past fifty years. At the same time, they also believe the federal government has important work to do on tough problems such as providing health care access for the poor. These respondents still see room for improvement across a range of issues.

As expected from the earlier discussion of ideology and demography, the academics disagreed on importance by discipline and demographics. Economists were the least likely to define issues as important, followed by political scientists, historians, and sociologists. The sociologists disagreed with the economists on the importance of thirty-three of the fifty endeavors; with political scientists,

Most Important Endeavors to Continue

Endeavor	Percent[a]
Increase arms control and disarmament	81
Expand and protect the right to vote	73
Increase health care access for low-income families	73
Improve air quality	68
Promote financial security in retirement	68
Improve elementary and secondary education	67
Increase health care access for older Americans	63
Provide assistance for the working poor	63
Ensure safe food and drinking water	61
Reduce workplace discrimination	61

a. Respondents rating endeavor as a very important issue.

AFP PHOTO/POOL/ALLEN EYESTONE

Bush or Gore? Antiquated voting machines created an electoral impasse in the state of Florida after the 2000 presidential election. Here, voting officials in West Palm Beach examine a damaged ballot to see which candidate, if any, would get the vote.

on twenty-five; and with historians, on fifteen, taking the more liberal position in all cases.

For example, sociologists were much more likely to see the need to continue reducing nuclear weapons: 95 percent rated the issue as very important, compared to 86 percent of historians, 73 percent of economists, and just 69 percent of political scientists. Sociologists were also more likely to see the problems in all facets of poverty: 85 percent rated health care access for low-income Americans as very important, compared to 74 percent of political scientists, 72 percent of historians, and 62 percent of economists.

Sociologists were not always the ones most worried, however. Among the top ten concerns, historians took the strongest position on the right to vote, and all four disciplines were in close agreement on the importance of promoting financial security in retirement.

Although the disagreements obviously outnumbered the agreements, there were sixteen endeavors in which the four sets of respondents did find common ground, including the importance of promoting space exploration and reducing illegal drug use.

Degrees of Responsibility

The federal government's greatest priorities should also involve endeavors that are largely federal responsibilities. Simply stated, the federal government should reserve its greatest energies for problems that only it can solve.

These rankings appear to result from two different justifications for federal engagement. On the one hand, many respondents appear to view the federal government as the only level that can handle interstate problems such as air pollution, food safety, and airline safety. They also believe that the federal government is the only level that can and should mount a strong national defense, control immigration, and negotiate arms control. After all, state and local governments do not have armies, most do not have borders with other nations, and none have nuclear weapons.

Similarly, these respondents seem to believe that states, localities, nonprofits, and the private sector have the greater responsibility for helping victims of disaster, reducing crime, reducing welfare dependency, and renewing poor communities. Other traditional state and local priorities such as improving elementary and secondary education, increasing low-income housing, and improving mass transportation were also rated below the 40 percent mark on federal responsibility.

On the other hand, these respondents still believe that state and local government cannot be trusted to protect the right to vote, reduce workplace discrimination, reduce exposure to hazardous waste, or protect the wilderness. Nor do they believe that state and local governments can assemble a health care financing system to cover the elderly or poor, or find the political will to provide assistance for the working poor. Although some states such as California, Massachusetts, Minnesota, and Wisconsin have been leaders in set-

Smallest Responsibilities of the Next Half-Century

Endeavor	Percent[a]
Expand homeownership	7
Reduce illegal drug use	11
Stabilize agricultural prices	11
Devolve responsibility to the states	18
Increase market competition	21
Expand job training and placement	23
Reduce crime	25
Reduce dependency among welfare recipients	25
Promote and protect democracy	26
Develop and renew impoverished communities	27
Help victims of disaster	27

a. Respondents stating that the federal government has a large responsibility.

ting stringent environmental standards or making voting easier, these respondents appear to worry more about the states that have lagged behind, whether in helping the needy or enhancing the right to vote.

Not all of these ratings involved a rational distribution of responsibilities across the sectors, however. Respondents did not think the federal government had a very great responsibility for promoting democracy, for example, or for space exploration or devolving responsibility to the states. But if the federal government does not have responsibility for these three issues, then who does? Only the federal government has the resources for a space program, and only the federal government can devolve responsibilities to the states.

Government's Greatest Failures

Much as one can admire the effort to address difficult problems such as discrimination, pollution, or poverty, the federal government should pursue priorities that have at least some chance of success, which in turn implies at least some history of impact. Past failure was a recurring theme among academics who felt that the federal government should discontinue endeavors such as stabilizing agricul-

Largest Responsibilities of the Next Half-Century

Endeavor	Percent[a]
Increase arms control and disarmament	87
Expand and protect the right to vote	78
Strengthen the national defense	74
Promote financial security in retirement	67
Improve air quality	66
Increase health care access for low-income families	66
Strengthen the nation's airways system	62
Ensure safe food and drinking water	60
Protect the wilderness	58
Reduce exposure to hazardous waste	58
Reduce workplace discrimination	58
Increase health care access for older Americans	58
Control immigration	58
Provide assistance for the working poor	58

a. Respondents stating that the federal government has a large responsibility.

tural prices, devolving responsibilities to the states, and promoting and defending democracy from communism.

It is important to note, however, the failure question was only asked of academics who said an endeavor should be discontinued. As a result it is not clear whether this list would be the same for those who said each endeavor should be continued.

Top Priorities of the Next Fifty Years

Unlike the rankings of government's greatest achievements, which involved a mix of importance, difficulty, and success, it is much easier to rank the federal government's top priorities of the future. All one has to do is ask each respondent which endeavors should be a top priority and provide the list. This method obviously assumes that anyone who said an endeavor should not be continued would also say it should not be a top priority.

The lists illustrate two lessons about setting priorities for the future. First, past success—or lack thereof—can predict whether an

Ten Greatest Failures of the Past Half-Century

Endeavor	Percent[a]
Increase nuclear arms control and disarmament	82
Increase market competition	77
Reduce illegal drug use	74
Reduce dependency among welfare recipients	61
Control immigration	60
Develop and renew impoverished communities	58
Increase international economic development	57
Reduce exposure to hazardous waste	55
Expand foreign markets for U.S. goods	54
Increase the supply of low-income housing	54

a. Respondents stating that past efforts had failed.

endeavor is given top-priority status or not. The fact that the federal government has done so well in the past in promoting financial security in retirement, providing health care access for the elderly, improving air quality, and expanding the right to vote is no reason to stop these endeavors now, particularly when events such as the 2000 election impasse in Florida suggest that there is still work to be done. Yet the fact that the federal government also did well in strengthening the highway system, helping veterans readjust, and promoting space exploration is not cause for making these endeavors a priority. At least for these academics, the federal government has done enough in these areas.

Second, these respondents believe that the federal government has important work to do in addressing past failures. On the list of government's greatest achievements of the past half-century, increasing health care access for low-income families was rated number 34, improving elementary and secondary education was number 35, and providing assistance for the working poor was number 40, in large part because they all were so difficult to solve.

There were several significant differences between respondents who filled out the survey before and after September 11. Those who completed the survey after September 11 were more likely to give a

Top Priorities of the Next Half-Century

Endeavor	Percent[a]
Increase arms control and disarmament	66
Increase health care access for low-income families	59
Expand and protect the right to vote	54
Promote financial security in retirement	51
Provide assistance for the working poor	47
Improve air quality	44
Increase health care access for older Americans	43
Improve elementary and secondary education	42
Reduce workplace discrimination	40
Strengthen the national defense	36
Ensure safe food and drinking water	36

a. Respondents rating endeavor as a top priority.

higher priority to both arms control (69 percent after September 11 versus 56 percent before) and health care access for low-income Americans (61 percent versus 52 percent, respectively), probably because of heightened concerns about an unsafe world.

Post–September 11 respondents also gave a number of terrorism-related endeavors higher ratings as priorities: strengthen the nation's airways system (37 percent of post–September 11 respondents ver-

Lowest Priorities of the Next Half-Century

Endeavor	Percent[a]
Stabilize agricultural prices	2
Expand homeownership	4
Support veterans' readjustment and training	5
Promote space exploration	5
Increase market competition	6
Reduce illegal drug use	6
Devolve responsibility to the states	8
Strengthen the nation's highway system	10
Help victims of disaster	10
Reduce dependency among welfare recipients	13

a. Respondents rating endeavor as a top priority.

sus 16 percent of pre–September 11 respondents), ensure an adequate energy supply (32 percent versus 20 percent, respectively), enhance the nation's health care infrastructure (25 percent versus 13 percent), increase the stability of financial markets (20 percent versus 13 percent), enhance workplace safety (20 percent versus 11 percent), reduce crime (18 percent versus 8 percent), and help victims of disaster (11 percent versus 5 percent).

Finally, post–September 11 respondents were much more likely to mention the war on terrorism when asked whether there were any top priorities missing from the survey. Only 3 percent mentioned terrorism before September 11, compared to 15 percent afterward, making it the most frequently mentioned missing priority.

CONCLUSION

America faces two very different futures. One is hopeful, the other uncertain; one is bright with new achievement, the other clouded with questions about the nation's willingness to persevere.

The first future is one in which the nation's leaders are able to maintain the bipartisan spirit that marks so much of government's past achievement. It is one in which Congress and the president work together to forge consensus on the tough, important problems already known and to address the crises not yet imagined. It is also a future in which Congress, the president, and the public embrace the patient progress that has produced so much achievement in the past.

The second future is one in which Congress and presidents worry so much about their reelection and popularity that they demand immediate success or none at all. It is one in which young Americans continue to avoid government service for fear of dead-end careers and bureaucratic red tape, thereby robbing government of the talent it needs to succeed. It is also a future in which the nation's own leaders continue to demean government and its civic partners for not being able to do more and more with less and less.

It is not yet clear which future will emerge from the current crisis. What is clear is that future success demands strong, bipartisan leadership from both Congress and presidents, and public tolerance for the small steps that eventually add up to great impact. Continued progress demands raw political courage of the kind shown in so many of the past breakthroughs described in this book. Given its past record of success through periods of civil unrest, domestic terrorism, international anxiety, and its own political instability, it is hard to bet against the federal government. Although each generation must address its own challenges, some entirely new, others familiar, the American system of government has been mostly moving forward for more than two hundred years. Where there is a will, there has always been a way. The question for the future is whether the will exists. Thus far in this new era of uncertainty, the answer has been a resounding yes.

Government's Greatest Endeavors of the Past Half-Century

Advance Human Rights and Provide Humanitarian Relief
Improving social conditions abroad by protecting human rights and providing relief aid. Examples: United Nations charter, 1945; Comprehensive Anti-Apartheid Act, 1986; Kosovo intervention, 1999.

Contain Communism
Impeding the spread of communism. Examples: Aid to Greece and Turkey, 1947; North Atlantic Treaty, 1949; Korean and Vietnam Wars.

Control Immigration
Setting and enforcing standards on immigration; temporary admission; naturalization; and the removal of aliens. Examples: Immigration and Nationality Act (McCarran-Walter), 1952; Immigration and Nationality Act amendments, 1965; Immigration Reform and Control Act, 1986; Immigration Act, 1990.

Develop and Renew Impoverished Communities
Improving the quality of life in poor rural and urban areas. Examples: Appalachian Regional Development Act, 1965; Demonstration Cities Act, 1966.

Devolve Responsibilities to the States
Shifting power from the federal government to the states. Examples: State and Local Fiscal Assistance Act (general revenue sharing), 1972; Unfunded Mandate Reform Act, 1995; Personal Responsibility and Work Opportunity Reconciliation Act (welfare reform), 1996.

Enhance Consumer Protection
Creating safety standards and raising awareness of potential hazards. Examples: Amendments to Food, Drug and Cosmetics Act, 1962; Fair Packaging and Labeling Act, 1966; Consumer Product Safety Act, 1972.

Enhance the Nation's Health Care Infrastructure
Building medical treatment and research facilities. Examples: Hospital Survey and Construction Act, 1946; Mental Retardation Facilities Construction Act, 1963; Heart Disease; Cancer and Stroke amendments, 1965.

Enhance Workplace Safety
Reducing workplace hazards. Examples: Federal Coal Mine Health and Safety Act, 1969; Occupational Safety and Health Act, 1970.

Ensure an Adequate Energy Supply
Facilitating the development of domestic energy sources and promoting conservation. Examples: Atomic Energy Act, 1954; trans-Alaskan pipeline, 1973; Energy Policy and Conservation Act, 1975; Natural Gas Wellhead Decontrol Act, 1989.

Ensure Safe Food and Drinking Water
Establishing and enforcing food and water quality standards. Examples: Federal Insecticide; Fungicide and Rodenticide Act, 1947; Wholesome Meat Act, 1967; Safe Drinking Water Act, 1974.

Expand Foreign Markets for U.S. Goods
Reducing tariff and nontariff barriers to trade. Examples: Bretton Woods Agreement Act, 1945; General Agreement on Tariffs and Trade, 1947; Organization for Economic Cooperation and Development Treaty, 1961; North American Free Trade Agreement, 1993.

Expand Homeownership
Promoting ownership through home loans and mortgages. Examples: Housing Act, 1950 and 1959; Tax Reform Act, 1986.

Expand Job Training and Placement
Creating jobs and providing vocational training. Examples: Employment Act, 1946; Small Business Act, 1953; Economic Opportunity Act, 1964; Comprehensive Employment and Training Act, 1973; Job Training Partnership Act, 1982.

Expand the Right to Vote
Guaranteeing the right to vote for all Americans over age eighteen. Examples: Civil Rights Act, 1964; Twenty-fourth Amendment, 1964; Voting Rights Act, 1965; Twenty-sixth Amendment, 1971.

Improve Air Quality
Controlling air pollution and raising air quality standards. Examples: Clean Air Act, 1963; Motor Vehicle Pollution Control Act, 1965.

Improve Elementary and Secondary Education
Enhancing education from preschool through high school. Examples: National Defense Education Act, 1958; Elementary and Secondary Education Act, 1965; Head Start, 1967.

Improve Government Performance
Enhancing government efficiency. Examples: Civil Service Reform Act, 1978; Federal Managers' Financial Integrity Act, 1982; Chief Financial Officers Act, 1990; Government Performance and Results Act, 1993; Federal Acquisitions Streamlining Act, 1994.

Improve Mass Transportation
Developing improved urban mass transportation and railway systems. Examples: Urban Mass Transportation Act, 1964; Rail Passenger Service Act, 1970.

Improve Water Quality
Controlling water pollution and raising water quality standards. Examples: Water Pollution Control Act, 1948 and 1972; Water Quality Act, 1965 and 1987.

Increase Access to Postsecondary Education
Providing assistance for higher education through loans, grants, and fellowships; building and improving facilities. Examples: Higher Education Facilities Act, 1963; Higher Education Act, 1965.

Increase Arms Control and Disarmament
Limiting nuclear weapon development and use. Examples: Nuclear Test Ban Treaty, 1963; Nuclear Nonproliferation Treaty, 1969; SALT/ABM Treaty, 1972; Intermediate Range Nuclear Force Treaty, 1988.

Increase Health Care Access for Low-Income Families
Providing health insurance to poor Americans. Examples: Medicaid, 1965; Children's Health Insurance Program, 1997.

Increase Health Care Access for Older Americans
Providing health insurance to older Americans. Examples: Medicare, 1965; Catastrophic Health Insurance for the Aged, 1988.

Increase International Economic Development
Providing aid for development. Examples: Establishment of the International Bank for Reconstruction and Development under the Bretton Woods Agreement Act, 1945; Act for International Development, 1950; Peace Corps, 1961.

Increase Market Competition
Deregulating industries including airlines, banks, utilities, and telecommunications. Examples: Airline Deregulation Act, 1978; Gramm-Leach-Bliley Act (financial services overhaul), 1999.

Increase the Stability of Financial Institutions and Markets
Increasing access to financial market information; assisting ailing institutions and averting potential problems. Examples: Securities and Exchange Act, 1975; Insider Trading and Securities Fraud Enforcement Act, 1988; Financial Institutions Reform, Recovery and Enforcement Act, 1989.

Increase the Supply of Low-Income Housing
Developing new public housing and subsidizing rents in private units. Examples: Housing Act, 1949; Housing and Community Development Act, 1965 and 1974.

Maintain Stability in the Persian Gulf
Removing Iraqi forces from Kuwait in the 1991 Gulf war.

Make Government More Transparent to the Public
Increasing public access to government activity and reducing administrative abuse. Examples: Administrative Procedures Act, 1946; Freedom of Information Act, 1966 and 1974; Government in the Sunshine Act, 1976; Ethics in Government Act, 1978; Inspector General Act, 1978.

Promote Equal Access to Public Accommodations
Desegregating public facilities and requiring handicapped accessibility. Examples: Civil Rights Act, 1964; Open Housing Act, 1968; Americans with Disabilities Act, 1990.

Promote Financial Security in Retirement
Raising Social Security benefits, expanding the number of recipients, ensuring program's solvency, protecting private pensions, and encouraging individual savings for retirement. Examples: Social Security expansions; Supplemental Security Income program, 1972; Employment Retirement Income Security Act, 1974.

Promote Scientific and Technological Research
Supporting basic research and developing new technologies such as the Internet. Examples: National Science Foundation Act, 1950; Defense Advanced Research Projects Agency, 1958; Communications Satellite Act, 1962.

Promote Space Exploration
Developing the technology for a lunar landing and further space exploration. Examples: National Aeronautics and Space Administration Act, 1958; Apollo mission funding, 1962; funds for a manned space station, 1984.

Protect Endangered Species
Preventing loss of threatened species. Examples: Marine Mammal Protection Act, 1972; Endangered Species Act, 1973.

Protect the Wilderness
Safeguarding land from commercial and recreational development. Examples: Wilderness Act, 1964; Wild and Scenic Rivers Act, 1968; Alaska National Interest Lands Conservation Act, 1980.

Provide Assistance for the Working Poor
Raising the income of the working poor through tax credits, assistance with expenses, and a guaranteed minimum wage. Examples: Earned Income Tax Credit, 1975; Family Support Act, 1988; increases to the minimum wage.

Rebuild Europe after World War II
Supporting post–World War II economic recovery and political stability. Examples: Establishment of the International Monetary Fund under the Bretton Woods Agreement Act, 1945; Foreign Assistance Act, 1948; North Atlantic Treaty, 1949.

Reduce Crime
Increasing the number of law enforcement officers, strengthening penalties, controlling guns, and supporting prevention programs. Examples: Omnibus Crime Control and Safe Streets Act, 1968 and 1994; Brady Handgun Violence Prevention Act, 1993.

Reduce Disease
Preventing and treating disease through research, direct assistance, and regulation. Examples: Polio Vaccine Act, 1955; National Cancer Act, 1971.

Reduce Exposure to Hazardous Waste
Restoring the environment and managing hazardous waste. Examples: Resource Conservation and Recovery Act, 1976; Comprehensive Environmental Response, Compensation and Liability Act (Superfund), 1980.

Reduce Hunger and Improve Nutrition

Providing food assistance to children and adults. Examples: National School Lunch Act, 1946; Food Stamp Act, 1964; Special Supplemental Food Program for Women, Infants and Children (WIC), 1972.

Reduce the Federal Budget Deficit

Balancing the federal budget. Examples: Balanced Budget and Emergency Deficit Control Act (Gramm-Rudman-Hollings), 1985; Omnibus Budget Reconciliation Act, 1990 and 1993; Balanced Budget Act, 1997.

Reduce Workplace Discrimination

Prohibiting employers from discriminating on the basis of race, color, religion, gender, national origin, age, or disability. Examples: Equal Pay Act, 1963; Civil Rights Act, 1964; Age Discrimination Act, 1967; Americans with Disabilities Act, 1990.

Reform Taxes

Lowering tax rates. Examples: Revenue Act, 1964; Economic Recovery Tax Act, 1981.

Reform Welfare

Increasing self-sufficiency among welfare recipients. Examples: Omnibus Budget Reconciliation Act, 1981; Personal Responsibility and Work Opportunity Reconciliation Act, 1996.

Stabilize Agricultural Prices

Supporting crop prices, distributing surpluses, and controlling production. Examples: Agriculture Act, 1948 and 1961; Agriculture Trade Development and Assistance Act, 1954; Food Security Act, 1985.

Strengthen the Nation's Airways System

Creating and maintaining the air traffic control system and promoting the safety and development of the air transportation industry. Examples: Federal Airport Act, 1946; Airport and Airways Development Act, 1970.

Strengthen the Nation's Highway System
Building, improving, and maintaining the interstate highway system. Examples: Federal-Aid Highway Act, 1956; Intermodal Surface Transportation Efficiency Act, 1991.

Strengthen the National Defense
Building and modernizing the national defense. Examples: Authorization of tactical and strategic weapons systems; Department of Defense Reorganization Act, 1958; Goldwater-Nichols Department of Defense Reorganization Act, 1986.

Support Veterans' Readjustment and Training
Assisting veterans with their transition back to civilian life. Examples: Serviceman's Readjustment Act, 1944; New GI Bill Continuation Act (Montgomery GI Bill), 1987.

Ratings of Fifty Past Endeavors

Rank	Importance	%	Endeavors[a] Difficulty	%	Success	%
1	Expand the right to vote	89	Advance human rights and provide humanitarian relief	66	Rebuild Europe after World War II	82
2	Rebuild Europe after World War II	80	Increase arms control and disarmament	65	Expand the right to vote	61
3	Increase health care access for low-income families	78	Reduce workplace discrimination	53	Strengthen the nation's highway system	40
4	Reduce workplace discrimination	78	Develop and renew impoverished communities	52	Contain communism	36
5	Promote equal access to public accommodations	78	Contain communism	50	Promote equal access to public accommodations	34
6	Increase arms control and disarmament	78	Reduce crime	48	Reduce the federal budget deficit	33
7	Improve elementary and secondary education	75	Reduce the federal budget deficit	45	Support veterans' readjustment and training	29
8	Ensure safe food and drinking water	73	Reform welfare	43	Strengthen the national defense	26
9	Improve water quality	72	Increase international economic development	41	Increase health care access for older Americans	24
10	Improve air quality	72	Improve mass transportation	41	Promote financial security in retirement	23
11	Reduce hunger and improve nutrition	72	Improve air quality	40	Reduce disease	23
12	Increase health care access for older Americans	70	Promote equal access to public accommodations	39	Maintain stability in the Persian Gulf	21
13	Reduce disease	65	Improve elementary and secondary education	38	Promote space exploration	20

#					
14	Reduce exposure to hazardous waste	63	Rebuild Europe after World War II	38	Promote scientific and technological research
15	Improve mass transportation	61	Control immigration	36	Expand homeownership
16	Advance human rights and provide humanitarian relief	60	Increase health care access for low-income families	34	Expand foreign markets for U.S. goods
17	Provide assistance for the working poor	60	Promote space exploration	34	Increase access to postsecondary education
18	Promote financial security in retirement	60	Reduce exposure to hazardous waste	34	Ensure safe food and drinking water
19	Ensure an adequate energy supply	56	Expand the right to vote	34	Increase market competition
20	Enhance workplace safety	56	Ensure an adequate energy supply	32	Reduce workplace discrimination
21	Increase access to postsecondary education	53	Improve water quality	31	Increase the stability of financial institutions and markets
22	Enhance consumer protection	51	Improve government performance	29	Reduce hunger and improve nutrition
23	Increase the supply of low-income housing	50	Reduce disease	29	Enhance consumer protection
24	Develop and renew impoverished communities	49	Provide assistance for the working poor	27	Stabilize agricultural prices
25	Protect the wilderness	49	Make government more transparent to the public	27	Enhance workplace safety
26	Promote scientific and technological research	48	Increase the supply of low-income housing	26	Improve water quality
27	Strengthen the nation's airways system	47	Protect endangered species	25	Protect endangered species
28	Enhance the nation's health care infrastructure	47	Maintain stability in the Persian Gulf	25	Improve air quality
29	Increase international economic development	46	Enhance workplace safety	23	Protect the wilderness

(continued)

	Endeavors[a]					
Rank	Importance	%	Difficulty	%	Success	%
30	Make government more transparent to the public	46	Expand foreign markets for U.S. goods	22	Enhance the nation's health care infrastructure	8
31	Reduce crime	45	Increase health care access for older Americans	20	Reform taxes	8
32	Support veterans' readjustment and training	40	Enhance consumer protection	20	Strengthen the nation's airways system	6
33	Protect endangered species	38	Expand job training and placement	20	Increase international economic development	5
34	Reduce the federal budget deficit	36	Protect the wilderness	19	Ensure an adequate energy supply	5
35	Increase the stability of financial institutions and markets	36	Enhance the nation's health care infrastructure	19	Increase arms control and disarmament	4
36	Improve government performance	33	Ensure safe food and drinking water	19	Devolve responsibility to the states	4
37	Expand job training and placement	33	Reform taxes	18	Control immigration	3
38	Contain communism	32	Promote financial security in retirement	16	Increase health care access for low-income families	3
39	Reform welfare	31	Increase the stability of financial institutions and markets	16	Provide assistance for the working poor	3
40	Strengthen the nation's highway system	30	Stabilize agricultural prices	13	Make government more transparent to the public	3
41	Strengthen the national defense	28	Reduce hunger and improve nutrition	13	Reduce exposure to hazardous waste	3
42	Expand foreign markets for U.S. goods	28	Strengthen the nation's airways system	11	Reduce crime	3
43	Maintain stability in the Persian Gulf	24	Devolve responsibility to the states	11	Reform welfare	3

Rank	Endeavor	Rank	Endeavor	Rank	Endeavor	%
44	Stabilize agricultural prices	18	Strengthen the national defense	11	Improve elementary and secondary education	2
45	Expand homeownership	18	Increase market competition	11	Expand job training and placement	2
46	Reform taxes	17	Increase access to postsecondary education	9	Improve mass transportation	1
47	Promote space exploration	16	Promote scientific and technological research	7	Advance human rights and provide humanitarian relief	1
48	Control immigration	15	Support veterans' readjustment and training	6	Improve government performance	1
49	Increase market competition	13	Strengthen the nation's highway system	4	Develop and renew impoverished communities	<1
50	Devolve responsibility to the states	8	Expand homeownership	4	Increase the supply of low-income housing	0

a. Percentages are given for the number of respondents who rated each endeavor as very important, very difficult, and very successful. However, specific rank is based on overall placement of each endeavor on a four-point scale running from least (1) to most (4) important, difficult, and successful.

APPENDIX C

Ratings of Fifty
Future Endeavors

Rank	Continuation	%	Importance	%	Federal responsibility	%	Priority	%
					Endeavors[a]			
1	Improve air quality	98	Increase arms control and disarmament	81	Increase arms control and disarmament	87	Increase arms control and disarmament	66
2	Increase arms control and disarmament	97	Expand and protect the right to vote	73	Expand and protect the right to vote	78	Increase health care access for low-income families	59
3	Reduce disease	97	Increase health care access for low-income families	73	Strengthen the national defense	74	Expand and protect the right to vote	54
4	Ensure safe food and drinking water	97	Improve air quality	68	Promote financial security in retirement	67	Promote financial security in retirement	51
5	Strengthen the nation's airways system	96	Promote financial security in retirement	68	Improve air quality	66	Provide assistance for the working poor	47
6	Improve water quality	96	Improve elementary and secondary education	67	Increase health care access for low-income families	66	Improve air quality	44
7	Make government more transparent to the public	96	Increase health care access for older Americans	63	Strengthen the nation's airways system	62	Increase health care access for older Americans	43
8	Enhance consumer protection	96	Provide assistance for the working poor	63	Ensure safe food and drinking water	60	Improve elementary and secondary education	42
9	Protect the wilderness	96	Ensure safe food and drinking water	61	Protect the wilderness	58	Reduce workplace discrimination	40
10	Reduce exposure to hazardous waste	95	Reduce workplace discrimination	61	Reduce exposure to hazardous waste	58	Ensure safe food and drinking water	36
11	Expand and protect the right to vote	95	Improve water quality	57	Reduce workplace discrimination	58	Strengthen the national defense	36
12	Promote scientific and technological research	94	Reduce exposure to hazardous waste	56	Increase health care access for older Americans	58	Reduce exposure to hazardous waste	35

#	Goal		Goal		Goal		Goal	
13	Increase health care access for low-income families	94	Reduce disease	55	Control immigration	58	Improve water quality	33
14	Increase health care access for older Americans	94	Reduce hunger and improve nutrition	54	Provide assistance for the working poor	58	Strengthen the nation's airways system	31
15	Promote financial security in retirement	94	Strengthen the nation's airways system	52	Balance federal budget	56	Reduce hunger and improve nutrition	31
16	Ensure equal access to public accommodations	93	Ensure an adequate energy supply	50	Make government more transparent to the public	56	Reduce disease	31
17	Provide assistance for the working poor	93	Advance human rights and provide humanitarian relief	49	Improve water quality	55	Ensure an adequate energy supply	29
18	Enhance workplace safety	93	Strengthen the national defense	48	Ensure equal access to public accommodations	51	Protect the wilderness	27
19	Reduce workplace discrimination	93	Protect the wilderness	48	Improve government performance	50	Balance the federal budget	27
20	Increase the stability of financial institutions and markets	93	Increase access to postsecondary education	47	Reduce hunger and improve nutrition	48	Ensure equal access to public accommodations	26
21	Improve government performance	92	Ensure equal access to public accommodations	47	Reduce disease	48	Increase access to postsecondary education	26
22	Advance human rights and provide humanitarian relief	92	Promote scientific and technological research	46	Expand foreign markets for U.S. goods	43	Improve mass transportation	25
23	Support veterans' readjustment and training	92	Improve mass transportation	45	Ensure an adequate energy supply	43	Advance human rights and provide humanitarian relief	24
24	Protect endangered species	92	Increase the stability of financial institutions and markets	40	Enhance consumer protection	42	Promote scientific and technological research	23

(continued)

Rank	Continuation	%	Importance	%	Federal responsibility	%	Priority	%
					Endeavors[a]			
25	Help victims of disasters	92	Enhance consumer protection	39	Protect endangered species	42	Enhance the nation's health care infrastructure	22
26	Strengthen the nation's highway system	91	Enhance the nation's health care infrastructure	37	Increase the stability of financial institutions and markets	42	Expand foreign markets for U.S. goods	21
27	Reduce hunger and improve nutrition	91	Enhance workplace safety	37	Advance human rights and provide humanitarian relief	42	Develop and renew impoverished communities	20
28	Increase access to post-secondary education	91	Increase the supply of low-income housing	37	Support veterans' readjustment and training	41	Increase the supply of low-income housing	20
29	Control immigration	91	Expand foreign markets for U.S. goods	36	Enhance workplace safety	39	Make government more transparent to the public	19
30	Strengthen the national defense	89	Make government more transparent to the public	36	Improve mass transportation	38	Control immigration	18
31	Ensure an adequate energy supply	88	Increase international economic development	36	Promote scientific and technological research	36	Increase international economic development	18
32	Increase international economic development	88	Balance the federal budget	35	Improve elementary and secondary education	36	Increase the stability of financial institutions and markets	18
33	Expand foreign markets for U.S. goods	88	Reduce crime	35	Increase international economic development	36	Enhance consumer protection	17
34	Promote space exploration	86	Develop and renew impoverished communities	35	Reform taxes	35	Reform taxes	17

	Goal		Goal		Goal		Goal	
35	Improve mass transportation	85	Expand job training and placement	32	Increase access to postsecondary education	34	Promote and protect democracy	15
36	Enhance the nation's health care infrastructure	84	Control immigration	31	Strengthen the nation's highway system	32	Expand job training and placement	15
37	Improve elementary and secondary education	84	Protect endangered species	30	Promote space exploration	31	Reduce crime	15
38	Balance federal budget	83	Reduce dependency among welfare recipients	27	Increase the supply of low-income housing	31	Improve government performance	14
39	Reduce crime	80	Strengthen the nation's highway system	24	Enhance the nation's health care infrastructure	28	Protect endangered species	14
40	Develop and renew impoverished communities	79	Reform taxes	23	Develop and renew impoverished communities	27	Improve government performance	14
41	Expand job training and placement	78	Help victims of disasters	23	Help victims of disasters	27	Reduce dependency among welfare recipients	13
42	Reduce dependency among welfare recipients	76	Promote and protect democracy	23	Promote and protect democracy	26	Strengthen the nation's highway system	10
43	Increase the supply of low-income housing	76	Improve government performance	22	Reduce crime	25	Help victims of disasters	10
44	Expand homeownership	67	Increase market competition	16	Reduce dependency among welfare recipients	25	Devolve responsibility to the states	8
45	Increase market competition	63	Devolve responsibility to the states	13	Expand job training and placement	23	Increase market competition	6
46	Reform taxes	61	Reduce illegal drug use	12	Increase market competition	21	Reduce illegal drug use	6
47	Reduce illegal drug use	61	Support veterans' readjustment and training	12	Devolve responsibility to the states	18	Support veterans' readjustment and training	5

(continued)

			Endeavors[a]					
Rank	Continuation	%	Importance	%	Federal responsibility	%	Priority	%
48	Stabilize agricultural prices	59	Promote space exploration	11	Reduce illegal drug use	11	Promote space exploration	5
49	Promote and protect democracy	55	Expand homeownership	11	Stabilize agricultural prices	11	Expand homeownership	4
50	Devolve responsibility to the states	54	Stabilize agricultural prices	8	Expand homeownership	7	Stabilize agricultural prices	2

a. Percentages for the number of respondents who said an endeavor should be continued are rounded to the higher whole number, while rankings are based on fractions. In addition, although percentages are given for the number of respondents who rated each endeavor as very important, a large federal responsibility, and a top priority, the specific rank in each column is based on overall placement of each endeavor on a three-point scale: least (1) to most (3) important, small (1) to large (3) responsibility, and minor (1) to top (3) priority.

Further Reading

GENERAL RESOURCES

Aberbach, Joel. 1990. *Keeping a Watchful Eye: The Politics of Congressional Oversight.* Brookings.

Abraham, Henry J. 1999. *Justices, Presidents, and Senators*, revised ed. New York: Rowman and Littlefield.

Altshuler, Alan A., and Robert D. Behn. 1997. *Innovation in American Government.* Brookings.

Anderson, James E. 1990. *Public Policymaking: An Introduction.* Boston: Houghton Mifflin.

Berger, Peter L., and Richard John Neuhaus. 1996. *To Empower People: From State to Civil Society.* American Enterprise Institute.

Berry, Jeffrey M., Kent E. Portney, and Ken Thompson. 1993. *The Rebirth of Urban Democracy.* Brookings.

Brokaw, Tom. 1998. *The Greatest Generation.* Dell.

———. 1999. *The Greatest Generation Speaks.* Random House.

Cain, Louis P., and Jonathan R. T. Hughes. 1997. *American Economic History*, 5th ed. Boston: Addison-Wesley.

Conlon, Timothy. 1988. *New Federalism: Intergovernmental Reform from Nixon to Reagan.* Brookings

Delli Carpini, Michael X., and Scott Keeter. 1996. *What Americans Should Know about Politics and Why It Matters.* Yale University Press.

Derthick, Martha ,and Paul J. Quirk.1985. *The Politics of Deregulation.* Brookings.

Dionne, E. J., Jr. 1991. *Why Americans Hate Politics.* Simon and Schuster/ Touchstone.

Donahue, John D. 1997. *Disunited States: What's at Stake as Washington Fades and the States Take the Lead.* Basic Books.

Eckes, Alfred E., Jr. 1995. *Opening America's Market: U.S. Foreign Trade Policy Since 1776.* University of North Carolina Press.

Ehrenhalt, Alan. 1992. *The United States of Ambition: Politicians, Power, and the Pursuit of Office.* Times Books.

Elkins, Stanley, and Eric McKitrick. 1993. *The Age of Federalism.* New York: Oxford University Press,

Fenno, Richard. 1978. *Home Style: House Members in Their Districts.* Boston: Little, Brown.

Fesler, James, and Donald Kettl. 1991. *The Politics of the Administrative Process.* Chatham, N.J.: Chatham House.

Fiorina, Morris. 1989. *Congress: Keystone of the Washington Establishment,* 2d ed. Yale University Press.

Glynn, Caroll J., and others. 1999. *Public Opinion.* Boulder, Colo.: Westview Press.

Gore, Al. 1993. *From Red Tape to Results: Creating a Government That Works Better and Costs Less.* Report of the National Performance Review. Government Printing Office (GPO).

Heilbroner, Robert, and Lester Thurow. 1998. *Economics Explained: Everything You Need to Know about How the Economy Works and Where It's Going,* revised ed. Simon and Schuster.

Hess, Stephen. 2000. *The Little Book of Campaign Etiquette.* Brookings.

Howard, Christopher. 1997. *The Hidden Welfare State: Tax Expenditures and Social Policy in the United States.* Princeton University Press.

Katzmann, Robert A. 1997. *Courts and Congress.* Brookings.

Kegley, Charles W., and Eugene R. Wittkopf. 1995. *American Foreign Policy: Pattern and Process,* 5th ed. St. Martin's.

Kerwin, Cornelius. 1998. *Rulemaking: How Government Agencies Write Law and Make Public Policy,* 2d ed. Washington: CQ Press.

Kingdon, John W. 1984. *Agendas, Alternatives, and Public Policies.* Boston: Little, Brown.

Light, Paul C. 1997. *The Tides of Reform: Making Government Work, 1945–1995.* Yale University Press.

————. 1998. *The President's Agenda: Domestic Policy Choice from Kennedy to Clinton,* 3d ed. Johns Hopkins University Press.

————. 1999. *The True Size of Government.* Brookings.

————. 2000. *The New Public Service.* Brookings.

Loomis, Burdett. 1988. *The New American Politician: Ambition, Entrepreneurship, and the Changing Face of Political Life.* Basic Books.

Mayhew, David R. 1991. *Divided We Govern: Party Control, Lawmaking, and Investigations, 1946–1990.* Yale University Press.

Neustadt, Richard E. 1990. *Presidential Power,* 2d ed. Basic Books.

Nice, David C., and Patricia Fredericksen. 1994. *The Politics of Intergovernmental Relations.* Chicago: Nelson-Hall.

O'Brien, David M. 1991. *Constitutional Law and Politics: Civil Rights and Civil Liberties.* W. W. Norton.

————. 2000. *Storm Center: The Supreme Court in American Politics,* 5th ed. W. W. Norton.

Okun, Arthur M. 1975. *Equality and Efficiency: The Big Trade-Off.* Brookings.

O'Toole, Lawrence J., Jr. 1993. *American Intergovernmental Relations.* Washington: CQ Press.

Page, Benjamin, and Robert Shapiro. 1992. *The Rational Public: Fifty Years of Trends in America's Policy Preferences.* University of Chicago Press.

Rohr, John A. 1986. *To Run a Constitution: The Legitimacy of the Administrative State.* University of Kansas Press.

Schier, Steven E. 2000. *By Invitation Only: The Rise of Exclusive Politics in the United States.* University of Pittsburgh Press.

Schneier, Edward V., and Bertram Gross. 1993. *Legislative Strategy: Shaping Public Policy.* St. Martin's.

Sharp, James Roger. 1993. *American Politics in the Early Republic: The New Nation in Crisis.* Yale University Press.

Skoronek, Stephen. 1997. *The Politics That Presidents Make: Leadership from John Adams to Bill Clinton.* New York: Belnap Press.

Staayer, John, Robert Wrinkle, and J. L. Polinard. 1998. *State and Local Politics.* Boston: Bedford/St. Martin's.

Stimson, James. 1998. *Public Opinion in America: Moods, Cycles, Swings.* Boulder, Colo.: Westview Press.

Stone, Deborah. 1997. *Policy Paradox: The Art of Political Decisionmaking.* W. W. Norton.

Sundquist, James L. 1968. *Politics and Policy: The Eisenhower, Kennedy, and Johnson Years.* Brookings.

Tocqueville, Alexis de. 1988. *Democracy in America.* Harper Perennial.

Verba, Sidney, Kay Lehman Schlozman, and Henry Brady. 1995. *Voice and Equality: Civic Voluntarism in American Politics.* Harvard University Press.

Waldman, Stephen. 1995. *The Bill.* Penguin.

Weir, Margaret, ed. 1998. *The Social Divide: Political Parties and the Future of Activist Government.* Brookings.

Wilson, James Q. 1989. *Bureaucracy: What Government Agencies Do and Why They Do It.* Basic Books.

Wood, Gordon S. 1991. *The Radicalism of the American Revolution.* Vintage.

TOP TWENTY-FIVE ACHIEVEMENTS

Rebuild Europe after World War II

Arkes, Hadley. 1973. *Bureaucracy, the Marshall Plan, and the National Interest.* Princeton University Press.

Dulles, Allen W. 1993. *The Marshall Plan*. New York: Berg.

Ellwood, David W. 1992. *Rebuilding Europe: Western Europe, America and Postwar Reconstruction*. New York: Longman.

Fossedal, Gregory A. 1993. *Our Finest Hour: Will Clayton, the Marshall Plan, and the Triumph of Democracy*. Hoover Institution Press, Stanford University.

Hogan, Michael J. 1989. *The Marshall Plan: America, Britain, and the Reconstruction of Western Europe, 1947–1952*. Cambridge University Press.

Schain, Martin A. 2000. *The Marshall Plan Fifty Years After*. St. Martin's.

Trachtenberg, Stephen Joel. 2000. *The Marshall Plan from Those Who Made It Succeed*. New York: University Press of America.

Expand the Right to Vote

Abraham, Henry J., and Barbara A. Perry. 1998. *Freedom and the Court: Civil Rights and Liberties in the United States*, 7th ed. Oxford University Press.

Davidson, Chandler, and Bernard Grofman, eds. 1994. *Quiet Revolution in the South: The Impact of the Voting Rights Act, 1965–1990*. Princeton University Press.

Grofman, Bernard. 1990. *Voting Rights, Voting Wrongs: The Legacy of* Baker *v.* Carr. New York: Priority Press Publications.

Grofman, Bernard, and Chandler Davidson, eds. 1991. *Controversies in Minority Voting: The Voting Rights Act in Perspective*. Brookings.

Hudson, David Michael. 1998. *Along Racial Lines: Consequences of the 1965 Voting Rights Act*. New York: Peter Lang Publishing.

Keyssar, Alexander. 2000. *The Right to Vote: The Contested History of Democracy in the United States*. Basic Books.

Klinkner, Philip A., and Rogers M. Smith. 1999. *The Unsteady March: The Rise and Decline of Racial Equality in America*. University of Chicago Press.

Kousser, J. Morgan. 1999. *Colorblind Injustice: Minority Voting Rights and the Undoing of the Second Reconstruction*. University of North Carolina Press.

Lawson, Steven F. 2001. *Black Ballots: Voting Rights in the South, 1944–1969*. Fordham University Press.

O'Brien, David. 1999. *Constitutional Law and Politics: Civil Rights and Civil Liberties*. 4th ed. W. W. Norton.

Rogers, Donald W., and Christine Brendel Scriabine, eds. 1992. *Voting and the Spirit of American Democracy: Essays on the History of Voting and Voting Rights in America*. University of Illinois Press.

Sundquist, James L. 1968. *Politics and Policy: The Eisenhower, Kennedy, and Johnson Years.* Brookings.

Promote Equal Access to Public Accommodations

Brooks, Barbara J. 1996. *Getting Uncle Sam to Enforce Your Civil Rights.* U.S. Commission on Civil Rights.
Graham, Hugh Davis, ed. 1994. *Civil Rights in the United States.* Pennsylvania State University Press.
Grofman, Bernard. 1999. *Legacies of the 1964 Civil Rights Act: Race, Ethnicity, and Politics.* University Press of Virginia.
Katzmann, Robert A. 1986. *Institutional Disability: The Saga of Transportation Policy for the Disabled.* Brookings.
Klinkner, Philip A., and Rogers M. Smith. 1999. *The Unsteady March: The Rise and Decline of Racial Equality in America.* University of Chicago Press.
Loevy, Robert D., ed. 1997. *The Civil Rights Act of 1964: The Passage of the Law That Ended Racial Segregation.* State University of New York Press.
Pardeck, John T. 1998. *Social Work after the Americans with Disabilities Act: New Challenges and Opportunities for Social Service Professionals.* Wesport, Conn.: Greenwood Publishing.
Snyder, David A. 1998. *Americans with Disabilities Act.* Washington: Labor Relations Information System.
West, Jane, ed. 1996. *Implementing the Americans with Disabilities Act.* New York: Blackwell.
Whalen, Charles, and Barbara Whalen. 1985. *The Longest Debate: A Legislative History of the 1964 Civil Rights Act.* Santa Ana, Calif.: Seven Locks Press.
Williams, Juan. 1998. *Eyes on the Prize: America's Civil Rights Years.* Penguin.

Reduce Disease

Black, Kathryn. 1997. *In the Shadow of Polio: A Personal and Social History.* Cambridge, Mass.: Perseus Publishing.
Fujimura, Joan H. 1997. *Crafting Science: A Sociohistory of the Quest for the Genetics of Cancer.* Harvard University Press.
Harden, Victoria Angela. 1986. *Inventing the NIH: Federal Biomedical Research Policy, 1887–1937.* Johns Hopkins University Press.

Kluger, Richard. 1997. *Ashes to Ashes: America's Hundred-Year Cigarette War, the Public Health, and the Unabashed Triumph of Philip Morris.* Vintage.

Martin, Emily. 1995. *Flexible Bodies: Tracking Immunity in American Culture from the Days of Polio to the Age of AIDS.* Boston: Beacon Press.

Muraskin, William A. 1998. *The Politics of International Health: The Children's Vaccine Initiative and the Struggle to Develop Vaccines for the Third World.* State University of New York Press.

Peller, Sigismund. 1979. *Cancer Research Since 1900: An Evaluation.* Philadelphia: Philosophical Library.

Seavey, Nina Gilden, Paul Wagner, and Jane S. Smith. 1998. *A Paralyzing Fear: The Triumph over Polio in America.* TV Books.

Strickland, Stephen P. 1989. *Story of the NIH Grants Program.* New York: University Press of America.

Reduce Workplace Discrimination

Belton, Robert, and Dianne Avery. 1998. *Employment Discrimination Law: Cases and Materials on Equality in the Work Place.* West Publishing, College and School Division.

Fogel, Walter A. 1984. *Equal Pay Act: Implications for Comparable Worth.* Westport, Conn.: Greenwood Publishing.

Loevy, Robert D. 1990. *To End All Segregation: The Politics of the Passage of the Civil Rights Act of 1964.* New York: University Press of America.

Mansbridge, Jane. 1986. *Why We Lost the ERA.* University of Chicago Press.

O'Meara, Daniel P. 1989. *Protecting the Growing Number of Older Workers: The Age Discrimination in Employment Act.* Center for Human Resources, University of Pennsylvania.

Pellicciotti, Joseph M. 1989. *An Analysis of the Age Discrimination in Employment Act.* Alexandria, Va.: International Personnel Management Association.

Wallace, Phyllis A., and Annette M. LaMond. 1977. *Women, Minorities, and Employment Discrimination.* Lexington, Mass.: Lexington Books.

Walsh, James. 1995. *Mastering Diversity: Managing for Success under ADA and Other Anti-Discrimination Laws.* Santa Monica, Calif: Merritt Publishing.

Wolkinson, Benjamin W., and Block, Richard N. 1995. *Employment Law: The Workplace Rights of Employees and Employers.* Malden, Mass.: Blackwell.

Ensure Safe Food and Drinking Water

Greene, Janice L., Janet S. Hathaway, and Cuneo McKenna. 1989. *Regulation of Pesticides: FIFRA Amendments of 1988.* Washington: BNA Press.

League of Women Voters of the United States. 1989. *America's Growing Dilemma: Pesticides in Food and Water.*

Leonard, Barry, ed. 2001. *Implementing the Food Quality Protection Act.* Collingdale, Pa.: Diane Publishing.

Lewis, Scott Allan. 1996. *The Sierra Club Guide to Safe Drinking Water.* San Francisco: Sierra Club Books.

National Conference of State Legislatures. 1990. *Compliance with the Safe Drinking Water Act.* Denver, Colo.

Obmascik, Mark. 2001. *A Consumer's Guide to Drinking Water: Where It Comes From, How It's Made Safe and What to Do if Something Goes Wrong.* Washington: American Water Works.

Shapton, David A. 1991. *Principles and Practices for the Safe Processing of Foods.* Woburn, Mass.: Butterworth-Heinemann.

Strengthen the Nation's Highway System

Boske, Leigh B. 1999. *Case Studies of Multimodal/Intermodal Transportation Planning Methods, Funding Programs and Projects.* Austin, Tex.: Lyndon B. Johnson School of Public Affairs.

Bourne, Russell. 1995. *Americans on the Move: A History of Waterways, Railways, and Highways.* Golden, Colo.: Fulcrum Publishing.

D'Amato, Alfonse M., ed. 2000. *Federal Mass Transit Program and the Reauthorization of the Intermodal Surface Transportation Efficiency Act (ISTEA): Congressional Hearing.* Collingdale, Pa.: Diane Publishing.

Frumkin, Norman. 1998. *Tracking America's Economy,* 3d ed. Armonk, N.Y.: M. E. Sharpe.

Kaszynski, William. 2000. *The American Highway: The History and Culture of Roads in the United States.* Jefferson, N.C.: McFarland.

Lewis, Tom. 1999. *Divided Highways: Building the Interstate Highways, Transforming American Life.* Viking Penguin.

Rose, Mark H. 1990. *Interstate: Express Highway Politics, 1939–1989.* University of Tennessee Press.

Increase Health Care Access for Older Americans

Aaron, Henry J., and Robert D. Reischauer. 1999. *Setting National Priorities: The 2000 Election and Beyond.* Brookings.

Blevins, Sue A. 2001. *Medicare's Midlife Crisis*. Cato Institute.

Century Foundation. 2001. *Medicare Tomorrow: The Report of the Century Foundation Task Force on Medicare Reform.*

Handler, Joel F. 1995. *The Poverty of Welfare Reform*. Yale University Press.

Henderson, Tim M., and Linda R. Lipson. 1997. *Primary Care for Older Americans: A Primer*. Denver, Colo.: National Conference of State Legislatures.

Himelfarb, Richard. 1995. *Catastrophic Politics: The Rise and Fall of the Medicare Catastrophic Coverage Act of 1988*. Pennsylvania State University Press.

Howard, Christopher. 1997. *The Hidden Welfare State: Tax Expenditures and Social Policy in the United States*. Princeton University Press.

Light, Paul C. 1993. *Still Artful Work: The Continuing Politics of Social Security Reform*. McGraw-Hill.

Marmor, Theodore R. 2000. *The Politics of Medicare*. Hawthorne, N.Y.: Aldine de Gruyter.

Matthews, Joseph L., and Dorothy M. Berman. 1999. *Social Security, Medicare, and Pensions*. Berkeley, Calif.: Nolo.

Pauly, Mark V., William L. Kissick, and Laura E. Roper, eds. 1989. *Lessons from the First 20 Years of Medicare: Research Implications for Public and Private Sector Policy*. University of Pennsylvania Press.

Peterson, Mark A., ed. 2001. *Medicare Intentions, Effects, and Politics*. Duke University Press.

Poen, Monte M. 1996. *Harry S. Truman versus the Medical Lobby: The Genesis of Medicare*. University of Missouri Press.

Rappaport, Anna M., and Sylvester J. Schieber, eds. 1993. *Demography and Retirement: The Twenty-First Century*. Westport, Conn.: Greenwood Publishing.

Skocpol, Theda. 1997. *Boomerang: Health Care Reform and the Turn against Government*. New York: W.W. Norton,

White, Joseph. 2001. *False Alarm: Why the Greatest Threat to Social Security and Medicare Is the Campaign to "Save" Them*. Johns Hopkins University Press.

Reduce the Federal Budget Deficit

Bryant, Ralph C. 1994. *Consequences of Reducing the U.S. Budget Deficit*. Brookings.

Cain, Louis P., and Jonathan R. T. Hughes. 1997. *American Economic History*, 5th ed. Boston: Addison-Wesley.

Evans, Gary R. 1997. *Red Ink: The Budget, Deficit, and Debt of the U.S. Government.* San Diego: Academic Press.

Heilbroner, Robert, and Lester Thurow. 1998. *Economics Explained: Everything You Need to Know about How the Economy Works and Where It's Going,* revised ed. Simon and Schuster.

Kosters, Marvin H., ed. 1992. *Fiscal Politics and the Budget Enforcement Act.* New York: University Press of America.

Makin, John H. 1990. *Balancing Act: Debt, Deficits, and Taxes.* New York: University Press of America.

Reams, Bernard D., Jr., and Margaret H. McDermott. 1986. *Deficit Control and the Gramm-Rudman-Hollings Act: History of the Balanced Budget and Emergency Deficit Control Act of 1985 (P.L. 99-177).* Buffalo, N.Y.: William S. Hein.

Reams, Bernard D., and Faye L. Couture, eds. 1994. *Revenue Reconciliation Act of 1990: Title XI Omnibus Budget Reconciliation Act of 1990, Public Law 101-508.* Buffalo, N.Y.: William S. Hein.

Schick, Allen. 2000. *The Federal Budget: Politics, Policy, Process,* 2d ed. Brookings.

Shaviro, Daniel. 1997. *Do Deficits Matter?* Chicago: University of Chicago Press,

Promote Financial Security in Retirement

Aaron, Henry J., and others. 2001. *Perspectives on the Draft Interim Report of the President's Commission to Strengthen Social Security.* Center on Budget and Policy Priorities and the Century Foundation.

Campbell, John Y., and Martin Feldstein, eds. 2001. *Risk Aspects of Investment-Based Social Security Reform.* University of Chicago Press.

Costa, Dora L. 2000. *The Evolution of Retirement: An American Economic History, 1880–1990.* University of Chicago Press.

Elmendorf, Douglas W. 2001. *Fiscal Policy and Social Security Policy during the 1990s.* Cambridge, Mass.: National Bureau of Economic Research.

Haber, Carole, and Brian Gratton. 1994. *Old Age and the Search for Security: An American Social History.* Indiana University Press.

Light, Paul C. 1993. *Still Artful Work: The Continuing Politics of Social Security Reform.* McGraw-Hill.

Lyon, Andrew B. 2000. *Comparing Current Social Security Reform Proposals.* American Association of Retired Persons, Public Policy Institute.

Patashnik, Eric M. 2000. *Putting Trust in the U.S. Budget: Federal Trust Funds and the Politics of Commitment.* New York: Cambridge University Press.

Razin, Assaf. 2001. *The Aging Population and the Size of the Welfare State.* Cambridge, Mass.: National Bureau of Economic Research.

Schieber, Sylvester J., and John B. Shoven. 1999. *The Real Deal: The History and Future of Social Security.* Yale: University Press.

Shaviro, Daniel N. 2000. *Making Sense of Social Security Reform.* University of Chicago Press.

Improve Water Quality

Adler, Robert W., Diane M. Cameron, and Jessica Landman. 1993. *The Clean Water Act 20 Years Later.* Washington: Island Press.

Barzilay, Joshua I., Winkler Weinberg, and J. William Eley. 1999. *The Water We Drink: Water Quality and Its Effects on Health.* Rutgers University Press.

Hunter, Susan, and Richard W. Waterman. 1996. *Enforcing the Law: The Case of the Clean Water Acts.* Armonk, N.Y.: M. E. Sharpe.

Lis, James. 1992. *Clean Water—Murky Policy.* St. Louis: Center for the Study of American Business.

Moyle, Petrea. 1999. *Pesticides in Ground Water: Will the EPA's New Regulation Decrease Health Risks?* AEI-Brookings Joint Center for Regulatory Studies.

Novotny, Vladimir, and Harvey Olem. 1997. *Water Quality: Prevention, Identification, and Management of Diffuse Pollution.* John Wiley and Sons.

Perry, James A., and Elizabeth Vanderklein. 1996. *Water Quality: Management of a Natural Resource.* Boston: Blackwell Science.

Portney, Paul R., and Robert N. Stavins, eds. 2000. *Public Policies for Environmental Protection.* Washington: Resources for the Future.

Support Veterans' Readjustment and Training

Bennett, Michael J. 1999. *When Dreams Come True: The GI Bill and the Making of Modern America.* Dulles, Va.: Brassey's.

Blechman, Barry M. 1976. *The Use of the Armed Forces as a Political Instrument.* Brookings.

Greenberg, Milton. 1997. *The GI Bill: The Law That Changed America.* New York: Lickle.

Levitan, Sar A. 1973. *Swords into Plowshares: Our GI Bill.* Salt Lake City: Olympus.

President's Commission on Veterans' Pensions .1956. *A Report on Veterans' Benefits in the United States.* GPO.

Richardson, Robert Brooks. 1968. *Transferring Military Experience to Civilian Jobs: A Study of Selected Air Force Veterans.* U.S. Department of Labor, Manpower Administration.

Skocpol, Theda. 1995. *Protecting Soldiers and Mothers: The Political Origins of Social Policy in the United States.* Harvard University Press.

Promote Scientific and Technological Research

Bowler, Peter J. 1993. *The Norton History of the Environmental Sciences.* W. W. Norton.

Davies, Kevin. 2000. *Cracking the Genome: Inside the Race to Unlock Human DNA.* New York: The Free Press.

England, J. Merton. 1982. *A Patron for Pure Science: The National Science Foundation's Formative Years, 1945–57.* National Science Foundation.

Richelson, Jeffrey T. 2001. *America's Space Sentinels: DSP Satellites and National Security.* University Press of Kansas.

Rothman, Barbara Katz. 2001. *The Book of Life: A Personal and Ethical Guide to Race, Normality, and the Implications of the Human Genome Project.* Boston: Beacon Press.

Smith, Brian H. 2000. *Controlling Our Destinies: The Human Genome Project from Historical, Philosophical, Social, and Ethical Perspectives.* University of Notre Dame Press.

Contain Communism

Abramowitz, Morton, ed. 2000. *Turkey's Transformation and American Policy.* New York: Century Foundation Press.

Carpenter, Ted Galen, ed. 1990. *NATO at 40: Confronting a Changing World.* Cato Institute.

Clemens, Clay, ed. 1997. *NATO and the Quest for Post-Cold War Security.* St. Martin's Press.

Crabb, Cecil V. 1992. *Invitation to Struggle: Congress, the President, and Foreign Policy,* 4th ed. Washington: CQ Press.

Daalder, Ivo H. 1999. *NATO at 50: The Summit and Beyond.* Brookings.

Golden, James R., and others. 1989. *NATO at Forty: Change, Continuity, and Prospects.* Boulder, Colo.: Westview Press.

Gordon, Philip H. 2001. *NATO Enlargement: Moving Forward.* Brookings.

Kull, Steven, and I. M. Destler. 1999. *Misreading the Public: The Myth of a New Isolationism.* Brookings.

Kuniholm, Bruce Robellet. 1980. *The Origins of the Cold War in the Near East: Great Power Conflict and Diplomacy in Iran, Turkey, and Greece.* Princeton University Press.

Rush, Kenneth. 1979. *NATO at 30: A Symposium on the Future of the Alliance.* Washington: Atlantic Council of the United States.

Spanier, John, and Steven W. Hook. 1998. *American Foreign Policy since World War II.* Washington: CQ Press.

Stearns, Monteagle 1992. *Entangled Allies: U.S. Policy toward Greece, Turkey, and Cyprus.* New York: Council on Foreign Relations Press.

Stern, Laurence M. 1977. *The Wrong Horse: The Politics of Intervention and the Failure of American Diplomacy.* Times Books.

Trubowitz, Peter. 1998. *Defining the National Interest: Conflict and Change in American Foreign Policy.* University of Chicago Press.

Urwin, Derek W. 1995. *The Community of Europe, A History of European Integration since 1945,* 2d ed. New York: Longman.

Improve Air Quality

Bryner, Gary C. 1995. *Blue Skies, Green Politics: The Clean Air Act of 1990 and Its Implementation.* Washington: CQ Press.

Crout, J. Richard, and others. 1983. *Public Policy, Science, and Environmental Risk: Addresses.* Presented at a Brookings Institution workshop, February 28, 1983.

Foreman, Christopher H., Jr. 1998. *The Promise and Peril of Environmental Justice.* Brookings.

Godish, Thad. 1997. *Air Quality.* Boca Raton, Fla.: Lewis.

Graham, Mary. 1999. *The Morning after Earth Day: Practical Environmental Politics.* Brookings and the Governance Institute.

Lave, Lester B. 1981. *Clearing the Air: Reforming the Clean Air Act,* staff paper. Brookings.

Lutter, Randall W. 2001. *Assessing Benefits of Ground Level Ozone: What Role for Science in Setting National Air Quality Standards?* AEI-Brookings Joint Center for Regulatory Studies.

Manne, Alan Sussmann. 2001. *US Rejection of the Kyoto Protocol: The Impact on Compliance Costs and Emissions.* AEI-Brookings Joint Center for Regulatory Studies.

Melnick, R. Shep. 1983. *Regulation and the Courts: The Case of the Clean Air Act.* Brookings.

Pearson, John K. 2001. *Improving Air Quality: Progress and Challenges for the Auto Industry.* Washington: Society of Automotive Engineers.

Sieg, Holger, and others. 2000. *Estimating the General Equilibrium Benefits of Large Policy Changes: The Clean Air Act Revisited.* Cambridge, Mass.: National Bureau of Economic Research.

Sunstein, Cass R. 1999. *Is the Clean Air Act Unconstitutional?* AEI-Brookings Joint Center for Regulatory Studies.

Transportation Research Board. 1976. *Assessing Transportation-Related Air Quality Impacts.* National Research Council.

U.S. Department of Health, Education, and Welfare. 1968. *Progress in the Prevention and Control of Air Pollution.* Report of the Secretary of Health, Education, and Welfare to the Congress of the United States. GPO.

White, Lawrence J. 1982. *The Regulation of Air Pollutant Emissions from Motor Vehicles.* American Enterprise Institute.

Enhance Workplace Safety

Bartel, Ann P. 1982. *OSHA Enforcement, Industrial Compliance and Workplace Injuries.* Cambridge, Mass.: National Bureau of Economic Research.

————. 1985. *Predation through Regulation : The Wage and Profit Impacts of OSHA and EPA.* Cambridge, Mass.: National Bureau of Economic Research.

Chelius, James Robert. 1977. *Workplace Safety and Health: The Role of Workers' Compensation.* American Enterprise Institute.

Gray, Wayne B. 1984. *The Impact of OSHA and EPA Regulation on Productivity.* Cambridge, Mass.: National Bureau of Economic Research.

————. 1991. *Do OSHA Inspections Reduce Injuries? A Panel Analysis.* Cambridge, Mass.: National Bureau of Economic Research.

Hartnett, John. 1995. *OSHA in the Real World: How to Maintain Workplace Safety While Keeping Your Competitive Edge.* Santa Monica, Calif.: Merritt.

Mitchell, Olivia S. 1982. *The Labor Market Impact of Federal Regulation: OSHA, ERISA, EEO and Minimum Wage.* Cambridge, Mass.: National Bureau of Economic Research.

Strengthen the National Defense

Adelman, Kenneth L. 1990. *The Defense Revolution: Strategy for the Brave New World by an Arms Controller and an Arms Builder.* San Francisco, Calif.: ICS Press.

Barnet, Richard J. 1990. *The Rockets' Red Glare: When America Goes to War.* Simon and Schuster.

Blackwell, J. A., Jr., and Barry M. Blechman. 1990. *Making Defense Reform Work.* Dulles, Va.: Brassey's.

Carter, Ashton B., and William J. Perry. 1999. *Preventive Defense: A New Security Strategy for America.* Brookings.

Clark, Asa A., and Peter W. Chiarelli. 1984. *The Defense Reform Debate: Issues and Analysis.* Johns Hopkins University Press.

Dellums, Ronald V. 1983. *Defense Sense: The Search for a Rational Military Policy.* Cambridge, Mass.: Ballinger.

O'Hanlon, Michael. 2000. *Technological Change and the Future of Warfare.* Brookings.

Pillar, Paul. 2001. *Terrorism and U.S. Foreign Policy.* Brookings.

Record, Jeffrey. 1988. *Beyond Military Reform: American Defense Dilemmas.* Dulles, Va.: Brassey's.

Rehnquist, William H. 1999. *All the Laws but One: Civil Liberties in Wartime.* Vintage.

Reduce Hunger and Improve Nutrition

Berg, Alan. 1973. *The Nutrition Factor: Its Role in National Development.* Brookings.

Bergmann, Barbara R. 1996. *Saving Our Children from Poverty: What the United States Can Learn from France.* New York: Russell Sage.

Besharov, Douglas J., and Peter Germanis. 2000. *Rethinking WIC: An Evaluation of the Women, Infants, and Children Program.* AEI Press.

Bremner, Robert Hamlett. 1971. *Children and Youth in America: A Documentary History.* Harvard University Press.

Huston, Aletha C., ed. 1991. *Children in Poverty: Child Development and Public Policy.* Cambridge University Press.

McGuire, Judith S., and Barry M. Popkin. 1990. *Helping Women Improve Nutrition in the Developing World: Beating the Zero Sum.* World Bank.

Office of Human Services Policy. 1998. *Aid to Families with Dependent Children: The Baseline.* Office of the Assistant Secretary for Planning and Evaluation, U.S. Department of Health and Human Services.

Osmani, S. R., ed. 1992. *Nutrition and Poverty.* Clarendon Press.

Skocpol, Theda. 1995. *Protecting Soldiers and Mothers: The Political Origins of Social Policy in the United States.* Harvard University Press.

Increase Access to Postsecondary Education

Bound, John. 1999. *Going to War and Going to College: Did World War II and the G.I. Bill Increase Educational Attainment for Returning Veterans?* Cambridge, Mass.: National Bureau of Economic Research.

Cohen, Arthur M. 1998. *The Shaping of American Higher Education: Emergence and Growth of the Contemporary System.* New York: Jossey-Bass.

Gordon, Michael, and Shelby Keiser, eds. 2000. *Accommodations in Higher Education under the Americans with Disabilities Act.* New York: Guilford.

Hartman, Robert W. 1974. *Financing the Opportunity to Enter the "Educated Labor Market."* Brookings.

Lucas, Christopher J. 1996. *American Higher Education.* Boston: St. Martin's.

Munger, Frank J. 1962. *National Politics and Federal Aid to Education.* Syracuse University Press.

Rudolph, Frederick. 1994. *The American College and University: A History.* University of Georgia Press.

Thomas, Norman C. 1975. *Education in National Politics.* New York: D. McKay.

Williams, Mary Frase. 1978. *Government in the Classroom: Dollars and Power in Education.* New York: Academy of Political Science.

Enhance Consumer Protection

Basara, Lisa Ruby, and Michael Montagne. 1997. *Searching for Magic Bullets: Orphan Drugs, Consumer Activism, and Pharmaceutical Development.* Binghamton, N.Y.: Haworth Press.

Beales, J. Howard. 1993. *State and Federal Regulation of National Advertising.* AEI Press.

Clancy, Katherine L. 1988. *Consumer Demands in the Marketplace: Public Policies Related to Food Safety, Quality, and Human Health.* Proceedings of a workshop held in Airlie, Va., October 27–29, 1986. National Center for Food and Agricultural Policy, Resources for the Future.

Fritschler, A. Lee, and James M. Hoefler. 1995. *Smoking and Politics: Policy Making and the Federal Bureaucracy.* Prentice-Hall.

Lave, Lester B. 1981. *The Strategy of Social Regulation: Decision Frameworks for Policy.* Brookings.

Meier, Kenneth J., E. Thomas Garman, and Lael R. Keiser. 1997. *Regulation and Consumer Protection: Politics, Bureaucracy and Economics.* Mason, Ohio: Dame.

Turner, James S. 1970. *The Chemical Feast: The Ralph Nader Study Group Report on Food Protection and the Food and Drug Administration.* New York: Grossman.

Vogel, David. 1989. *When Consumers Oppose Consumer Protection.* St. Louis, Mo.: Center for the Study of American Business, Washington University.

———. 1995. *Trading Up: Consumer and Environmental Regulation in a Global Economy.* Harvard University Press.

Expand Foreign Markets for U.S. Goods

Atwood, Margaret, William Greider, and Ralph Nader. 1993. *The Case against Free Trade: GATT, NAFTA and the Globalization of Corporate Power.* Berkeley, Calif.: North Atlantic Books.

Black, Stanley W. 1991. *A Levite among the Priests: Edward M. Bernstein and the Origins of the Bretton Woods System.* Boulder, Colo.: Westview Press.

Bordo, Michael D. 1993. *The Gold Standard, Bretton Woods and Other Monetary Regimes: A Historical Appraisal.* National Bureau of Economic Research.

Cameron, Maxwell A. 2000. *The Making of NAFTA: How the Deal Was Done.* Cornell University Press.

Giovannini, Alberto. 1992. *Bretton Woods and Its Precursors: Rules versus Discretion in the History of International Monetary Regimes.* National Bureau of Economic Research.

Jackson, John Howard. 2000. *The Jurisprudence of GATT and the WTO.* Cambridge University Press.

James, Harold. 1996. *International Monetary Cooperation since Bretton Woods.* Oxford University Press.

Kenen, Peter B. 1997. *Managing the World Economy: Fifty Years after Bretton Woods.* Institute for International Economics.

MacArthur, John R. 2000. *The Selling of "Free Trade": NAFTA, Washington, and the Subversion of American Democracy.* New York: Hill and Wang.

Robert, Maryse. 2000. *Negotiating NAFTA: Explaining the Outcome in Culture, Textiles, Autos, and Pharmaceuticals.* University of Toronto Press.

Rockenbach, Leslie J. 2001. *The Mexican-American Border: NAFTA and Global Linkages.* New York: Routledge.

Schaefer, Brett. 2001. *The Bretton Woods Institutions: History and Reform Proposals.* Heritage Foundation.

Increase the Stability of Financial Institutions and Markets

Calavita, Kitty. 1997. *Big Money Crime: Fraud and Politics in the Savings and Loan Crisis.* University of California Press.

Congressional Budget Office. 1993. *Resolving the Thrift Crisis.* GPO.

Cottrell, Allin F., John H. Wood, and Michael S. Lawlor, eds. 1995. *The Causes and Costs of Depository Institution Failures.* New York: Kluwer Academic.

Macey, Jonathan R. 1991. *Insider Trading: Economics, Politics, and Policy.* AEI Press.

Malloy, Michael P. 1992. *The Regulation of Banking: Cases and Materials on Depository Institutions and Their Regulators.* Cincinnati, Ohio: Anderson.

Manz, William H. 2001. *Legislative History of the Gramm-Leach-Bliley Act: Public Law No. 106-102.* Buffalo: William S. Hein.

Robinson, Michael A. 1990. *Overdrawn : The Bailout of American Savings.* Dutton.

Spellman, Lewis J. 1982. *Depository Firm and Industry: Theory, History and Regulation.* Academic Press.

Increase Arms Control and Disarmament

Badash, Lawrence. 1995. *Scientists and the Development of Nuclear Weapons: From Fission to the Limited Test Ban Treaty, 1939–1963.* Amherst, N.Y.: Prometheus Books.

Dean, Jonathan. 1997. *Options and Opportunities: Arms Control and Disarmament for the 21st Century.* United Nations Association of the United States of America.

Duffy, Gloria, ed. 1982. *Intermediate-Range Nuclear Forces in Europe: Issue and Approaches.* Center for International Security and Cooperation.

Genest, Mark A. 1995. *Negotiating in the Public Eye: The Impact of the Press on the Intermediate-Range Nuclear Force Negotiations.* Stanford University Press.

Hackel, Erwin, and Gotthard Stein, eds. 2000. *Tightening the Reins: Towards a Strengthened International Nuclear Safeguards System.* Berlin and New York: Springer.

Heftman, Jeffery M. 1997. *An Evaluation of the Chemical Weapons Convention and the U.S. National Interest.* Arms Control, Disarmament, and International Security Program, University of Illinois.

Kintner, William R., and Robert L. Pfaltzgraff Jr., eds. 1973. *SALT: Implications for Arms Control in the 1970s.* University of Pittsburgh Press.

Labrie, Roger P., ed. 1979. *SALT Hand Book: Key Documents and Issues, 1972–1979.* American Enterprise Institute.

Lafferranderie, Gabriel, and Daphne Crowther, eds. 1997. *Outlook on Space Law over the Next 30 Years: Essays Published for the 30th Anniversary of the Space Treaty.* New York: Kluwer Law.

Scheinman, Lawrence. 1987. *The International Atomic Energy Agency and World Nuclear Order.* Johns Hopkins University Press.

Shelton, Frank H. 1992. *Reflections of a Nuclear Weaponeer: The Limited Test Ban Treaty, 1963.* Des Moines: Shelton Enterprises.

Williams, Robert C., and Philip L. Cantelon, eds. 1984. *The American Atom: A Documentary History of Nuclear Policies from the Discovery of Fission to the Present, 1939–1984.* University of Pennsylvania Press.

Wittner, Lawrence S. 1993. *The Struggle against the Bomb.* Stanford University Press.

Protect the Wilderness

Bowes, Michael D. 1989. *Multiple-Use Management: The Economics of Public Forestlands.* Resources for the Future.

Caldwell, Lynton Keith. 1998. *The National Environmental Policy Act: An Agenda for the Future.* Indiana University Press.

Chasek, Pamela S., ed. 2000. *The Global Environment in the Twenty-First Century: Prospects for International Cooperation.* Brookings.

Harvey, Mark W. 2000. *A Symbol of Wilderness: Echo Park and the American Conservation Movement.* University of Washington Press.

Huber, Peter W. 1999. *Hard Green: Saving the Environment from the Environmentalists: A Conservative Manifesto.* Basic Books.

Lemons, John, ed. 1997. *National Environmental Policy Act: Readings from the Environmental Professional.* Malden, Mass.: Blackwell Science.

Nash, Roderick Frazier. 2001. *Wilderness and the American Mind.* Yale University Press.

Oates, Wallace E., ed. 1992. *The Economics of the Environment.* New York: Elgar.

Wheat, Frank. 1998. *California Desert Miracle: The Fight for Desert Parks and Wilderness.* El Cajon, Calif.: Sunbelt Publications.

Promote Space Exploration

Beattie, Donald A. 2001. *Taking Science to the Moon: Lunar Experiments and the Apollo Program.* Johns Hopkins University Press.

Bilstein, Roger E. 1989. *Orders of Magnitude: A History of the NACA and NASA, 1915–1990.* NASA SP-4406. GPO.

Bromberg, Joan Lisa. 1999. *NASA and the Space Industry.* Johns Hopkins University Press.

Burrows, William E. 2000. *The Infinite Journey: Eyewitness Accounts of NASA and the Age of Space.* Discovery Books.

Launius, Roger D. 1994. *NASA: A History of the U.S. Civil Space Program.* Melbourne, Fla.: Krieger.

Launius, Roger D., John M. Logsdon, and Robert W. Smith, eds. 2000. *Reconsidering Sputnik: Forty Years since the Soviet Satellite.* New York: Routledge.

Logsdon, John M. 1995. *Exploring the Unknown: Selected Documents in the History of the US Civilian Space Program.* Vol. 1, *Organizing for Exploration.* NASA SP-4218. GPO.

———. 1996. *Exploring the Unknown: Selected Documents in the History of the US Civilian Space Program.* Vol. 2, *External Relationships.* NASA SP-4407. GPO.

———. 1998. *Exploring the Unknown: Selected Documents in the History of the US Civilian Space Program.* Vol. 3, *Using Space.* NASA SP-4407. GPO.

Spangenburg, Ray, and Diane Moser. 2000. *The History of NASA.* New York: Watts Franklin.

Swanson, Glen E. 1999. *Before This Decade Is Out . . .: Personal Reflections on the Apollo Program.* NASA SP-4223. GPO.

White, Irvin L. 1970. *Decision-Making for Space: Law and Politics in Air, Sea, and Outer Space.* Purdue University Studies.

Index

Medicare, 44, 46, 63, 84, 99–100
Medicare Act (*1965*), 2, 4, 29, 96, 98–99
Mental Retardation Facilities Construction Act (*1963*), 16
Middle Income Student Assistance Act (*1978*), 26
Migration and Refugee Assistance Act (*1962*), 11
Military: bases, 43, 102; budget, 131–33; reorganization, 133; research, 33
Miller, Cheryl, 79
Mine Safety Act (*1952*), 16–17
Mining: miner safety, 16–17, 127; strip mining control and reclamation, 35
Monopolies, 28
Motor voter law, 22, 73
Muller v. *Oregon,* 85
Mutual Security Act (*1957*), 27
Mutually assured destruction (MAD) theory, 152

Nader, Ralph, 91, 140
National Aeronautics and Space Administration (NASA), 33–34, 121, 160–62
National Association for the Advancement of Colored People (NAACP), 74–75, 163
National Cancer Institute, 83
National Commission on Social Security Reform, 107
National Council of Senior Citizens, 98
National Council on Health Planning and Development, 16
National Defense Education Act (*1958*), 23, 139
National Institute of Allergy and Infectious Diseases, 83
National Institute on Aging, 83

National Institutes of Health (NIH), 83, 121
National Mass Transportation Assistance Act (*1974*), 24
National Organization for Women (NOW), 163
National Park Service, 155
National School Lunch Act (*1946*), 39, 134
National Science Foundation (NSF), 33, 118–21
National Science Foundation Act (*1950*), 33, 118
National Security, U.S. Commission on, 174
National Security Act (*1947*), 10
National Security Council (NSC), 10
National Transportation Safety Board, 42
National Voter Registration Act (*1993*), 22, 73
National Wild and Scenic Rivers System, 156, 157–58
National Wilderness Preservation System, 34
National Wildlife Refuge System, 34
Nineteenth Amendment, 21
Nixon, Richard: arms treaties, 153; environmental protection, 108, 110; new federalism, 14–15; occupational safety and health, 129
North American Free Trade Agreement (NAFTA), 20, 146
North Atlantic Treaty Organization (NATO), 12
North Korea, 12
NSFNet, 121
Nuclear Nonproliferation Treaty, 26, 153
Nuclear power, 17–18
Nuclear Regulatory Commission, 18